Poverty Wasn't Painful

DEPRESSION RECOLLECTIONS OF EASTERN OREGON RANCH LIFE

by

Elaine Dahl Rohse

PORTLAND • OREGON
INKWATERPRESS.COM

Cover note:
Hidden in the cluster of trees on the Schafer place along the North Fork of the John Day, is the old ranch house. Faintly discernible in the distance is flat-topped Johnny Cake Mountain on the right, and Neal Butte on the left.

The columns in *Poverty Wasn't Painful*—in exact or revised form—first appeared in the *News-Register* of McMinnville, OR. Special thanks goes to Jeb Bladine, publisher, for this republication right.

Copyright © 2007 by Elaine Dahl Rohse

Cover and interior design by Masha Shubin
Cover photo by Louann Rohse

www.inkwaterpress.com

ISBN-13 978-1-59299-322-2
ISBN-10 1-59299-322-2

Publisher: Inkwater Press

Printed in the U.S.A.
All paper is acid free and meets all ANSI standards for archival quality paper.

Table of Contents

Acknowledgements

Everlasting thanks to my incomparably patient and helpful husband, Homer, who audited every word of "Poverty Wasn`t Painful." To our son, Mitch, who showed me the way with his book "Land-Use Planning in Oregon," and helped at every step in unraveling the electronic maze. To our daughter-in-law, Louann Rohse, a dynamo cheering section, whose photos were used on cover and back of the book.

Thanks galore to Jeb Bladine, publisher of the *McMinnville News-Register* in which most of the "Poverty Wasn`t Painful" columns first appeared as "Through Rohse Colored Glasses" — a column he named more than 30 years ago when it first appeared in that newspaper. Thanks to Racheal Winter at the *News-Register* for her skillful editing of the columns that resulted in an occasional journalistic award, and to Lindsay Burt and crew at Inkwater Press for putting it all together.

My appreciation, too, to my brother, Jack Forrest and his wife Darlene — the last of the family at Monument — who keep the home fires burning.

I treasure, too, fond recollections of the people of Monument — now mostly gone. In a few instances the names of real Monument people are used, but many names are fictional.

Finally, thanks to you who said, "I like your eastern Oregon columns".

Such as Roger Heller and Bill Duncan.

This book is dedicated to all of you.

CHAPTER 1

Richer Because We Were Poorer

Our parents gave us many things: food, shelter, love, appreciation for the outdoors, a love of reading. But their biggest gift to us, I'm thinking, was poverty.

Just about all my friends were given the same gift. We grew up in the Depression. We were given the gift of being poor.

At the time, we did not see it as a gift — perhaps because we did not know that we were poor. Poor to us was being homeless and selling apples on a Portland street corner. We were poor in one respect only. We had no cash money.

We had a roof over our heads — albeit one lacking electricity and indoor plumbing. Never did we go hungry. If one lived on a ranch and was resourceful, one never was without food. We borrowed from nature — and never paid her back: her elderberries and wild gooseberries for pie and jelly, her dandelions for spring greens, her deer for year-round venison, her trout from Wall Creek and Board Creek, her huckleberries for cobbler.

Ranchers helped nature along. Gates and fence posts were made from tree limbs, a chicken house from logs. Housewives didn't buy yeast cakes for homemade bread. They made "starter" from potato water — potatoes grown in their garden. They made their own butter and "cultivated" cottage cheese on the back of the wood cookstove.

Packaged foods were not available. Biscuits, cakes and puddings were made from scratch. Prepared cereals that cost several dollars per box weren't on our cupboard shelves. That much money provided breakfast cereals for us for a month: hot oatmeal, farina or cornmeal mush every morning.

Always we had clothes to keep us warm, although shoes may have been scuffed and perhaps we had only one pair. If kids didn't wear out clothes, they were handed down to the next child in line. If there weren't younger children, outgrown clothes went to a family where there were.

Nature also kept us warm. Fallen trees on the ranch provided wood for wood-burning heater and cookstove. Ranchers strung their own line for battery-operated phones. A coal oil lamp provided light. Water came from a spring up on the hill. We had no credit cards and no bills arrived at our mailbox at the Monument post office the first of every month.

Gifts that the Depression gave us included patience and hope. We expected to work for that which we received so it behooved us to have a work ethic. If we didn't like things the way they were, it was up to us to do something about it.

Our poverty was not a state of mind. It was a bit like having a cold: annoying perhaps, while one was so afflicted, but not life-altering. And when one catches a cold it is not necessarily one's fault. We did not regard it as our fault that we chanced to grow up during a Depression.

As for housing, in those days a roof over one's head was the goal. Never did we foresee that a few generations hence, young married couples might start living in a home costing several hundred thousand dollars. As a young married couple, Homer, my husband, and I, paid $35 a month for our one-bedroom apartment.

A bride today may be carried over the threshold into a home that is interior-decorator complete, whereas in the Depression era it was hodge-podge decor: a handed-down table from Aunt Tabitha, to be sanded and refinished; a bedstead from Moe and Mabel whose kids had grown up and moved from home; and occasionally orange crates that temporarily did quite well.

When we added a patio to one home, we had a patio pouring party and guests did most of the work. It was a memorable event. When we went camping, we slept out for a night or two, then splurged by going to a motel. We stayed home weekends from camping and fishing to put in a lawn. If we wanted a self-defrosting refrigerator we saved and then went out and bought it. And all of these practices were Depression lessons.

In a sense, those of us who lived in the Depression were a bit like the pioneers who crossed the plains to Oregon — although certainly we were not the heroes that they were. But we were like them in that we had dreams and hopes. That too was an era that provided foundation for our country.

If we are handed gifts at the start, we lose the triumph of attainment. Growing up in a Depression was a gift in that it nourished dreams.

Another of its gifts was that it gave us resiliency. The things that we hoped for didn't necessarily come the next day, or the next month — but if one hung in there, they well could come.

It taught appreciation for that which we had — and to not always look toward the next material attainment. Acquisitions were not the rights of our society.

There is a 17th century saying: "When poverty comes in the door, love flies out the window." But of the people we then knew, far fewer marriages ended with divorce than in the present era.

The author J. C. Holland wrote, "Of all the advantages which come to any young man, I believe it is demonstrably true that poverty is the greatest." Those of us who were kids during the Depression have one regret. Our parents lamented that they could not give us everything: a sports car, Adidas, a letterman's sweater, a European trip for spring break.

If only we could tell them today that we lived in a golden age — perhaps the best ever — and that poverty was not a disservice, but a gift that they gave us.

CHAPTER 2

Outhouses — A Place to Dream

As with covered bridges and spotted owls something should be done to save the few remaining outdoor plumbing facilities.

They once dotted the American countryside, located discreetly at the rear of every farm or ranch house — often with matrimonial vines planted about in an attempt at disguise.

On our eastern Oregon cattle ranch, our outdoor plumbing faced away from the dirt road by which infrequent vehicles and unexpected visitors arrived. On nice days I left the door open. The landscape before me was junipers, mahogany and sagebrush.

At the top of the hill within my view was a rimrock formation that changed into intriguing shapes at different hours. Sometimes it was a castle in Spain that I would visit someday. Some days it was a skyscraper in the megalopolis where I would in the future make my mark.

Sometimes jackrabbits, not knowing I was within a mile, scurried along their trail that crossed the field in front of our facility. Sometimes noisy magpies perched nearby and scolded me for annoying their privacy.

Never was there a better place for daydreaming and thinking. Here, nearly a block from the house, voices from the rest of the family could not be heard, nor motherly admonition to hurry and get at the dishes.

When the temperature was agreeable, I used our outhouse as reading room. After our big Sears and Wards catalogs became outdated, they still served a purpose. In some of the neighboring ranch facilities these catalogs were mounted on the walls, but ours were left unmounted. Ours was a family of avid readers. With no regard for passing time, I became absorbed in car mufflers, fashions one season old and cosmetics that would make me that which I was not.

When money became more plentiful, these catalogs were discarded for store-bought bathroom tissue. I was sorry when that time came.

These outdoor facilities provided, too, a chance to be outdoors. Waking in the morning one bounded from the porch and ran for the love of movement.

When it snowed I liked breaking trail to our facility. My tracks gave me a sense of leaving my mark on the earth's white tablecloth.

Our health books in the fifth grade dealt with these outdoor plumbing facilities. The author strongly recommended not placing an outhouse at a higher level than the water supply, in order to prevent contamination.

After studying that unit in our health book, I mentally checked location of both outhouses and water source when I visited friends. While staying overnight with a girl friend I noted that their outhouse was located up the hill in back of the house, directly in line with their well below. During my stay I drank little water and long after that visit I feared I might become a second Typhoid Mary.

Even though ecologists today might oppose a move to save the few remaining outhouses, air pollution should be of slight concern to them. Ranchers in eastern Oregon dealt with that problem by dumping ashes from the woodstove down the facility.

Two things were a concern with regard to our outhouse. Black widow spiders relished such a place as a home and we feared the bite of a black widow almost as much as that of a rattlesnake. My concern was their unwillingness to play fair. They often did not establish residence where they could be seen.

Instead they preferred the underneath side of the seat. In order to be perfectly sure they were not living there one sometimes had to crane one's head through the opening in the boards to see whether black widows were present.

Rattlesnakes, which delighted in hanging around old buildings, were a concern, too. I feared they might slither along the underneath part of the seat and sneak up unexpectedly. I could cope with rattlesnakes at ground level but our outhouse was a different matter. My fears were for naught and at least no rattler ever accosted me that way.

I suppose that as I grew older I might have grumbled at the inconvenience of these facilities that today I view with nostalgia. But nostalgia is a warm and fuzzy companion.

And despite shiny modern bathrooms, with carpets that warm feet on wintery nights, I cannot imagine that today's facilities ever will be regarded with nostalgia.

Not many old outhouses are left. As with covered bridges and Victorian mansions, I hate to see them go.

I had no room of my own in our two-room house, but our outhouse served that purpose. Our outhouse was where I launched dreams.

CHAPTER 3

Kitchen Queen Bloomers Were the Style

If you've never worn bloomers made from a flour sack you probably weren't raised on an eastern Oregon cattle ranch during the Depression.

On our ranch we knew the flour-sack era well.

We bought our flour in 50-pound quantities. It came in a coarse cotton material sack.

The name — "Kitchen Queen" or whatever — was printed thereon. Sometimes the sack featured a colored picture — a beaming woman who had just baked a fine loaf of bread. The poundage, the miller and his location were printed on it, too.

People ate heartily on cattle ranches. Physical demands required big meals. We had pancakes every morning; sourdough biscuits the other two meals of the day. Five pounds of flour scarcely would have been worth the bother of bringing it home.

Once emptied those flour sacks were put to good use.

For one thing, they made fine dishtowels. Sometimes the fussier homemakers made an effort to bleach out that beaming lady and the other printing. But even without bleaching, after the dishtowels dozens of times hung on our wire clothesline exposed to eastern Oregon sun, the reminder began to fade.

The sacks were stitched intricately on all sides. If you were experienced, one snip of the scissors and a pull on the right string could unravel the stitching lickety-split. If one could not find the right string and the sack had to be unraveled stitch by stitch, it was the annoyance of the day. Hemmed, or unhemmed, those sacks made dishtowels that wore like iron. Even after the material became soft and thin and holes appeared they were not discarded. They then served as dust cloths, rags for washing windows, or a bandage for a skinned knee.

If winters were hard and additional hay had to be bought for the cattle for several successive years, flour sacks served as pillow cases. They were not nearly as soft as muslin. You did not enjoy burrowing your face into Kitchen Queen.

Horseback riders in those days deemed flour sacks as necessary as a woman does a purse. When we rode horseback to get the mail, or pick up groceries at the one general store in Monument, flour sacks went along, If I were designated to make the trip, Mother repeatedly reminded me to put the mail in the sack and tie it securely to the back of the saddle so I would not lose it on the way home. Coffee and other canned goods I bought at the store were slipped in a flour sack and tied to the other side of the saddle. Today's plastic bags wouldn't work well for that.

There was a knack to tying that flour sack on the saddle. A big knot was first tied in the top of the sack so it couldn't slip through the saddle strings.

Never did a rancher go deer hunting without taking flour sack along. If it was a successful hunt, venison heart and liver were tied therein. The dressed deer was laid across and tied in the saddle, and the victorious hunter walked home.

When we rode for cattle, lunches were tied in flour sacks. They contained nails, staples and hammer when Lynn "rode" fence.

Early summer when Gravenstein apples were ready at the Stubblefield ranch, Mattie Stubblefield tied enough for several pies in a flour sack and by horseback made her annual pilgrimage to visit Mother for the day.

There was another use for flour sacks. During the Depression they were used as material for nightwear and bloomers. Little girls did not then wear slacks or shorts to school, and sometimes when we played on the rings and swings and the more daring little girls hung by their knees from the bars, it was evident that Kitchen Queen had been used for such. The more fastidious mothers — if the family consumed sufficient flour — used only that portion of the sack without printing, carefully cutting away the proud Kitchen Queen.

I never had flour-sack nightwear or bloomers but that was because Mother was not a proficient seamstress. Busy as she was feeding the chickens, picking the peas, taking care of the chickens, cooking big meals, she had no time to make bloomers and pajamas for me.

I do not recall, however, that there was the slightest stigma attached to wearing Kitchen Queen underwear. There were more necessary things to buy, and cash was a scarce crop during the Depression.

I doubt that many little girls wear Kitchen Queen bloomers nowadays. Perhaps flour, when bought in those big quantities, no longer comes in cloth sacks. Perhaps, too, if those sacks are available, Americans would scoff at using them today.

CHAPTER 4

The Event of the Day — The Coming of the Mail

Mail is private these days. It's dropped in our box. We seldom may even see the mailman.

But in little towns all across America the coming of the mail once was the highpoint of the day. Our post office in Monument with its scant 100 ranchers and residents was the town's social spa.

Early afternoon, six days weekly, the mail arrived, brought from Kimberly by the "hired contractor" in his private vehicle. A U.S. mail truck didn't carry Monument's mail which daily, amounted usually to a couple of drab-colored canvas bags — not nearly full.

Our post office was no sturdy brick structure symbolizing reliability of U.S. mail. It was an unpainted wooden building divided down the middle by a wall of mailboxes. On the front of each box, arranged in a circle were letters of the alphabet, with an arrow to turn to the letters that were the combination for opening the box.

At a window, behind a grate, our postmaster — whoever of the Merrill family was on duty that day — sold stamps and money orders when not distributing the mail.

The post office was in front of the Merrill's home, which was handy because they didn't have to stay in the post office all day. When a rancher came to town it might be necessary for him to go to the house to rouse someone to come sell stamps. But when the "stage," as we called it, arrived, the postmaster hurried to the office to begin distribution.

People wrote letters then to keep in touch and a three-cent stamp sent it to its destination. The junk-mail era had not yet then arrived and to Monument residents all mail was important. It was inestimably better to get something in one's box than nothing at all.

Town people and those on the ranch not helping with haying or other seasonal jobs went to the office daily for the big event. By the time the mail arrived, about everyone in the area had gathered at our little post office. Out-of-towners mostly came by horseback — the horses tied to the fence, dozing in the sun — not much excited about the coming of the mail.

Monument had no newspapers of its own but the daily Oregonian and Portland Journal arrived in the mail sacks, as did our weekly newspaper: the Blue Mountain Eagle in Canyon City. Its most important news, as far as we were concerned, was the inside column headed "Monument" wherein we learned Jenny Butler was going to John Day Tuesday to get eyeglasses, or that John Strong was thrown from a horse and broke a leg.

We had other ways, too, of getting news: notices on the post office wall. So did the government. A notice advised residents whose income exceeded a given amount that they were liable for income tax and were required to sign their name on that sheet for all of Monument to see. Only one name appeared thereon: the name of our local garage owner. Those were Depression days. Ranchers at least weren't worried about income tax.

But the coming of the mail served as Monument's "own" newspaper. As the congregation awaited the distribution of the mail, local happenings were discussed and passed along, as we watched the little window on our mail box to see if mail was placed there. Immediately upon seeing such, it was pulled from the box to read — and become common knowledge to all. Pearl's mother in Gresham was not well. The Pembertons were coming from Portland to go hunting with Gorhams. Mary in Umatilla would visit her parents on Easter.

For those who had no letter, it helped a little to share in this community mail. Letters always were distributed first, then packages, and lastly newspapers. If shoes ordered from Montgomery Ward arrived, a card was placed in the box that advised, "Please ask for parcel at window." Packages were almost more fun to receive than letters, but all mail was a status symbol.

When no mail any longer appeared in the windows, those residents who certainly had expected something queried our postmaster, "Is the mail all out? I was expecting that package from Sears today." Or, "I surely expected a letter from Maria." The postmaster heard that every day, as if it were his fault that Maria did not write.

During school, it was my job to pick up the mail every day and bring it when I came home. In the summer, at our ranch I also was designee to go the mile and a half to town to get the mail.

I minded not in the least. If we were "keeping-up" a saddle horse, I rode Old Skinny or Bubbles. But often I walked, took my swimsuit and swam in the John Day with the kids who congregated there every afternoon. Then I'd collect the mail and head home. I hated it if nothing was in our box. Mother was disappointed when there was no mail. But even when nothing was in our box I brought home tidbits from other people's mail, and news about happenings in town, and of coming events as posted on the post office wall.

Nowadays, mail is a sterile thing. It's slipped into slots or mailboxes — and almost always something is there — whether it's news that we're getting close to winning a million, or someone thinks our house needs siding.

What fun it would have been if Grandma Gibson, or George Curtis, or Pearl, or anyone there in the little Monument post office, had learned he'd just won a two million dollar prize. The whole town would have celebrated.

If people won a prize like that today, they might not even run across the street and tell a neighbor. Mail is more private these days.

CHAPTER 5

It Was the Sport of Kids

In the last moments of twilight when the Blue Mountains up Hamilton way turned to dark silhouettes and the mourning doves called out good night, we kids bounded outdoors to meet for our evening games at Monument.

Monument had no street lights, but we wanted none for our game. Our favorite was Run Sheep Run.

Such games couldn't be played in modern-day towns. We needed Monument's unfenced backyards, where owners were not proprietary about property lines and back yards were dotted with outhouses, wood piles and little pens for chickens.

Run Sheep Run, an unstructured game with few rules, required little skill. An unsophisticated game not found today in game books, it accommodated kids of any age who on any given evening came out to play. Even kids who couldn't run very fast were not told they couldn't play and sent home.

The primary object of the game — which we players thought was a good one — was to entertain. Each team had a scout: an older fleeter kid. The little kids could not run fast enough to be scouts, and some were afraid to be by themselves in the dark, although the dark in Monument was not to be feared.

Once organized into two teams, each with a designated scout, one team took off across Monument's dark back yards. After an elapsed time, the other team followed. The object of the first team was to elude the team that followed. To help that team do so, its scout "scouted" to see whether the other group of kids was headed in our direction. If so, our scout hallooed off through the dark, "Run Sheep Run." We who were being pursued then knew that we were about to be "captured" and took off in a different direction.

Some nights, we were so evasive that the other team never found us. Finally, we would get tired and go home, thinking how funny it was that the other team was still out there searching.

Run Sheep Run was our favorite night game, but we also had daytime games. Hopscotch was one. Since Monument had no paved streets, we drew the hopscotch design in the dirt with a stick and then hunted for a little piece of wood, which from behind the line, was tossed into the "rooms," or spaces, in sequence. We then hopped to that area on one foot, retrieved the block and hopped out, hopefully never getting on the lines.

The first squares were easy if one kept his balance, but as one progressed farther into the squares, one had to be a pretty good hippety-hopper and a pretty good pitcher to get that little piece of wood into the proper area and not on the line.

Sometimes, we played Prisoner's Base, which is a game about as old as war itself. It wasn't our favorite, although we tended to think it was more entertaining than Ante Over, which was played by our forebears when mothers made balls out of bits of material and stuffed them with whatever was handy. Sometimes we kids played softball, not in teams but "work up." When there was an out, we moved up one position, and eventually became batter.

It was disappointing to work up to be batter and then on the first pitch, hit a piddling drive toward first base, be out and again have to go out in the field. You learned a lot about what softball positions you wanted to play. Catching wasn't my favorite. And although I liked to pitch, my deliveries were as uncontrolled as a helium balloon.

In homes at night, we kids got together when the weather didn't permit Run Sheep Run and played card games: Old Maid and Eights and Pig. Pig was a great game. After one became a pig three times, the player was then a hog. Anyone talking to a hog also became a hog. So a hog used all manner of trickery to get others to converse.

On wintery nights, our family played hearts and still does to this day, fuming because our son "runs" it, in part by dint of his playing against the computer and honing his skills. Mother and I played honeymoon bridge, a two-handed affair, and sometimes pinochle was our family game.

Geography was a favorite pastime when we rode in the car long distances. Undemanding as to intellect or age, we played it for miles as we went down the road. One started by giving the proper name of any geographic entity, such as Portland. Portland ends with a D, so the next player gives a geographic name that starts with a D — perhaps Denver, whereupon the next player must come up with a place name that starts with R, such as Rhode Island. We tried to think of place names ending in Z, because after Zaire, Zambia, Zanzibar, Zimbabwe and Zanesville, Z was hard to come by.

Hopscotch, Run Sheep Run and Prisoner's Base aren't played much anymore. Maybe that's because they don't involve circuitry. Nor do they do much to prepare one to become a pro or a winner of an athletic scholarship. Any scholarship we might have received was for academic work. Athletic scholarships for girls were unheard of.

But parents didn't know how lucky they were to have their children growing up in Monument and playing such games. We kids wandered around town at will, night or day, sometimes alone. We kids knew not the meaning of child molestation. No child was ever kidnapped in Monument. There were no strangers in Monument.

I'm glad that despite living in an unenlightened age, we did not have computer games that might have diverted us from Run Sheep Run.

For us unenlightened kids, that game was pretty exciting. Still fondly today, I remember Run Sheep Run.

CHAPTER 6

Our Battle Against Rattlers

Every summer we lived with rattlesnakes in eastern Oregon, as mindful of them as a hot stove.

Those rattlers though, usually played fair. We killed a lot more of them than they did of us. My friend's mother was bitten by a rattlesnake but she lived. And I knew of no death resulting from a rattlesnake bite in Grant County, whereas we humans kept track of how many snakes we killed during a season. If we killed more than a couple of dozen, we termed it a "bad year", not only bad for the snakes, of course, but bad for us to have a reptile population that dense.

Around Monument, we didn't just walk away from a rattler. We lived by an unwritten law: If we saw or heard a snake, we did our best to make a kill. But not every rattler seemed to have the goal of biting every rancher it encountered. In most cases, those snakes were willing to let anyone that much bigger have right of way.

Then, too, the rattler was neighborly in that it usually sounded its warning. And no lesson was needed to identify that sound. Not many other sounds came close to resembling it, although walking through dried sunflower leaves could cause one to jump frantically aside.

Further, our eastern Oregon landscape provided weapons for killing snakes: rocks. Usually plenty of them. And rocks, aimed always at the snake's head, could be thrown from a safe distance. If one chanced to carry a shotgun or .22, a rattlesnake had little chance of surviving, unless one were a rotten shot.

But when one hiked the eastern Oregon hills or went to the garden, one did not usually carry a firearm. Without rocks or a gun, there was little else in most areas with which to kill a snake. A sagebrush limb didn't readily kill a rattler, and blows then had to be administered at close range. Rattlers were tough hombres to kill, and we kids were instructed to be certain they were dead before we walked away, particularly if we wanted to remove the rattles from them after the kill.

If those rattles were especially big — great in number — we often collected them like prize marbles. Old-timers said that the snake's approximate age could be told by number of rattles: one per year and one for the end button. Although I no longer have the rattles to prove it, I am certain we killed snakes having 12 to 15 rattles, and those rattles were as collectible as mule deer trophy racks.

Rattlers also were friendlier than some snakes in other lands. In Africa, we saw snakes that, from a considerable distance, could spit in one's eyes, causing blindness. Rattlesnakes had to be near enough to chomp down on their prey with their two long tubular, upper teeth, backed up by their poison gland in the roof of the mouth. We occasionally met feisty rattlers, but not often did they take after us in pursuit.

Although rattlesnakes generally played fair, our parents nonetheless schooled us in reptilia. They warned that when killing a rattler to be alert to the possibility of a companion snake nearby. Snakes were said to often travel in pairs, and if one were intent on killing one snake, another then could easily make its move.

We kids, too, were told that after killing a snake, it was important to bury a rattler's head. Despite being dead, if stung by a hornet or yellow jacket, the poison from the snake could be transmitted to the next creature that insect stung.

Rattlesnakes had something else in their favor. They closely resembled the harmless blow snakes prevalent in Grant County. We kids knew that the heads of poisonous snakes were flatter and more bull-dogged in shape than those of nonpoisonous snakes, but if not side by side, identification was doubtful. Markings and colorations of the blow snakes and rattlers were so similar that never was I expert enough to tell rattler from blow snake by that alone. The tail, however — whether rattles or no rattles — provided precise identification, requiring, nonetheless, that the snake obligingly crawl into the open and reveal its tail.

Living with rattlesnakes helped to educate us about the snake's life-style. We learned to be particularly watchful for them around damp areas. Rattlers have no controlling system for body temperature and can't toler-ate prolonged exposure to sunlight, so they seek shady damp areas. When Mother picked raspberries in the garden, she was especially watchful for them. She cautiously checked to see if a raspberry bush harbored a rattler before reaching for the plump, red berries. One statistic advised that 98 percent of snake bites are on hands, forearms or below the knee, so one looked before one reached.

Even away from damp areas and the garden, we knew in which areas of our ranch we were most apt to see snakes. We suspected that the rimrocks to the west of the ranch house were home to a snake den, and as many as 2,000 snakes may inhabit a den. As many as 20 hatch in a single litter.

One Monument resident started a cottage craft as a result of those prevalent rattlesnakes. She discovered — although I do not know how that discovery came about — that the skeleton of the rattlesnake was comprised of many intricately shaped bones, and began making jewelry from them. In order to get a supply of bones, she took her husband and friends on snake hunts, then stewed up the snakes so that the flesh could be cleaned from the bones. Those who visited that household during the cooking insisted it smelled exactly like chicken, and those who tasted the cooked flesh said it was similar to chicken in taste.

Another nice thing about rattlers: Winter gave us a vacation from their presence. While they hibernated, eastern Oregon ranchers could accumu-late rock piles, the better to attack them come summer.

CHAPTER 7

Oil Lamps Did the Job

Sometimes Abraham Lincoln's fame seems attributable in part to his studying by fire light — as mentioned in about every one of his biographies, along with his being president and freeing the slaves.

I studied by coal oil lamp — although no biographer has yet made note of that fact. All activities after dark at eastern Oregon ranch houses, in the early 1930s, were lighted by kerosene lamps.

Those lamps did not operate with a switch and required considerable daily maintenance.

Coal oil was bought at Boyer's Cash Grocery in Monument. When our supply ran low, one had to remember to take to town the empty gallon jug. One had to be careful when bringing home that filled jug, to not have it in close proximity to flour or sugar. Sometimes our food had a faint taste of coal oil if it spilled down the jug's sides, or if the jug leaked a bit while bringing it home with other groceries on horseback.

In addition to filling the lamps — and a ranch wife would never have waited until dark to fill them — the wicks had to be trimmed. Although trimming off that part of the wick that had burned merely meant scissoring it straight across the top with the metal wick holder as guide, it was hard to get wicks perfectly straight. When the lamps were lit, the wicks were turned as high as possible to provide the most light. If they were uneven, and part of the flame touched the chimney, it was blackened with soot. An evening started badly when a pristine chimney ended up black with the first lighting.

If those chimneys then were washed in the dish water, the black soot broke up into pesky little chunks that got on pots and pans. Experienced ranch wives knew that a good way to clean chimneys was with newspapers. They took off the black and polished the chimney nicely.

Some ranchers used Aladdin lamps that gave more light than our simple coal oil version. But Mother, not having grown up with Aladdin lamps, was suspicious of them and feared they might explode.

Aladdin lamps had fragile mantles — little sacks — more delicate than wicks. The Aladdins also had to be pumped up, a procedure Mother much distrusted. So she opted for our kerosene operation, although the candlepower was less.

Our lamp lit the immediate surrounding area but did not light the far corners. When I practiced shorthand at night, it was with the lamp at my elbow, being careful not to knock over that lamp because of danger of fire.

Nor did a flick of a switch initiate light from that lamp. A wooden kitchen match worked best. We kept the matches in a handy little metal container given customers one Christmas by Boyer's Cash Store. It was mounted on the wall and the match box slid handily in, so that it was not necessary to open the box to take out a match.

Nor, of course, did a coal oil lamp turn off with a switch, but we were cautious as to how we blew them out. Mother taught us the proper way. One did not blow down into the chimney, but across the top, with the palm of the hand at the far side. I know not whether it was an old wives' tale, but blowing down into the chimney, we were told, might force the flame into the kerosene and cause a fire.

The more affluent ranchers had a lamp for every room in the house. Otherwise, when you wanted something in the kitchen and took the lamp from the living room to light your way, that left those family members in the living room in the dark.

We had another light on the ranch: the kerosene lantern, used for doing outside chores after dark. It had a handy handle so it could be carried around, and a metal top that fitted snugly over the chimney so the flame would not blow out.

If one looked out after dark, at our ranch in eastern Oregon, one saw no street lights or lights from other ranch homes. One might see one little light from the lantern, about as big as an apple, bobbing around down at the shed as Lynn fed the work horses and made sure they were properly tied for the night.

Coal oil lamps surely provided better light for studying than did Abraham Lincoln's firelight. But how much more miraculous is a light switch.

CHAPTER 8

Cleanliness — It's All Relative

In early days in eastern Oregon during the Depression it was not easy to be clean.

One did not soak in a steaming tub of bubble bath. As far as we knew, only one ranch house in the Monument area had a genuine bathtub.

The rest of us depended on round metal washtubs for getting bodies clean — a far from daily routine. It was helpful that neither we nor our friends were of the bathe-every-day cult, because we were not then aware of others' offensiveness.

Our bathtub also served as Mother's washtub. Her washing machine was on the porch. Few ranch houses then had utility rooms.

After clothes were washed in the washing machine, one piece at a time was urged through the wringer. It obligingly — or sometimes less obligingly if the garment was a large pair of overalls — displaced the water, flattening out the piece of clothing so it looked like a pancake.

The "pancake" then flopped into the metal tub filled with blue rinse water that tried to induce the wash to be white.

This big washtub, which hung on the back of the house when not in use and added little to the exterior aesthetics of a ranch house, importantly served also as bathtub.

In those days, bathing was not taken lightly. After a hard day of haying or a cold day of riding for cattle, one at 9:30 at night did not then decide that a hot, relaxing bath was the answer.

Baths took planning. One first had to provide for hot water that we could do in two ways. The big tub could be placed atop the cookstove, filled partly with water and heated to near the boiling point. The tub was then removed from the stove and just the correct amount of cold water added so that one did not leap out of the water when stepping into it, suffering scalded feet, or cool it so much that before the bath was over it was remindful of jumping into the John Day River before summer had warmed the waters.

If one bathed at night when water was heated in the tub on the stove, it was necessary to keep the wood fire burning, in which event one did not let the fire go out after supper. At 8:30 p.m., one did not suddenly decide to build a fire in the cookstove, fill the tub, place it on the stove, wait a lengthy period for it to heat and then have a luxurious bath.

Further, if one heated bath water in the tub on the cookstove, the system required that someone else be at the ranch house. One person could not singly lift the tub off the stove. One person held the handle on one side of the tub, and the helper took hold of the handle on the other side and the unwieldy tub was placed on the floor.

We did, however, have a backup method, but this took even more planning. We could make sure the reservoir on the side of the kitchen stove was filled hours before bathing, since water in it heated slowly. The reservoir water was then supplemented with boiling water from the teakettle. This combined reservoir water and teakettle of water did not provide bath water in which one might drown, but called more for sponge bath technique.

This method was advantageous in one respect: one did not have to carefully consider the law of displacement. If the tub was too full and one placed one's body in the tub, the displaced water then gushed onto the kitchen floor. Since every bather was duty bound to mop up the displaced water after the bath, we kids religiously observed the displacement rule. The kitchen was our designated bathing area, in part because of warmth. The wood-burning heater in the living room and the wood-burning cookstove in the kitchen were our only sources of heat, and when we bathed on wintery days, one wanted to be as near as possible to a source of heat. If a bather had forethought when he took the tub off the stove, he also filled the stove with wood so that, when the bath was completed, the still-burning fire was friendly.

When one bathed, there was still another challenge: the matter of privacy. If one desired privacy, one did not choose bath time when Mother was baking a cake. Or when my brother was studying at the kitchen table. Or when my stepfather was trying to bring a half-frozen lamb back to life on the open oven door.

But the greatest challenge for us bathers was agility: the agility required to fit all of one's body into a round container some 2 1/2 feet across. One stepped gingerly into the water, hoping it was neither too cold nor too hot. With one's feet in the bottom of the tub, one had to find space for the rest of the body.

To do so, it was necessary to sit down when the feet already were taking up a goodly portion. The rest of the body, wanting also to be clean, hoped to be in the water, so the less body one had, the better. If one's body was able to fit in the tub, there was still the problem of knees. With body and feet in the tub, the knees were bent sharply, extending above the top of the tub.

Further, in this position, it was difficult to reach all parts of the body, and if at this point it was discovered that the soap had not been placed adjacent to the tub, one considered having a soapless bath.

After one managed to immerse the lower torso of the body in the water there was another problem. There was so little room between body and the sides of the tub, it was a challenge to get the washcloth down into the water and to bring up enough water for cleaning purposes. If the soap was at hand and one's back was thoroughly soaped, it took diligence to keep the rinse water from going on the floor.

At that time, growing up and weighing less than a hundred pounds, the tub scarcely accommodated me. Looking back, what a challenge it must have been for adults; for my Mother and my 6-foot tall stepfather, who weighed some 230 pounds.

Thus it was that in those days in eastern Oregon it was hard to be clean. We had one consolation. Just as we did not know that we were poor in those Depression days because everyone else was, so too, with regard to bathing, one could say that we ranch families in the Monument area were all in the same boat or in the same washtub.

CHAPTER 9

The Catalogs of Our Dreams

Christmas and Fourth of July were favorite days of the year on our ranch in eastern Oregon, but close behind was the day the mail order catalogs arrived.

We loved those catalogs. They were our dream worlds. Montgomery Ward and Sears Roebuck, the dependables, occasionally were briefly challenged by such catalogs as National Bellas Hess. But the challengers were small fry compared to the two whoppers.

Early spring and fall, the big Wards and Sears catalogs, about two inches thick, arrived at the Monument post office. They came without charge. The prerequisite for being on their list was to have ordered the previous season. That was no problem in Monument. Our shopping town, John Day, was about 60 miles away. Although John Day had only about 600 people, it boasted features that were big city to us: movie theater, bank, drug and variety stores, and from time to time a doctor. A few miles on down the road, Prairie City had a hospital.

About the time we thought those catalogs should arrive, we began to tingle with impatience—at least we teen-agers did. There was something in the catalog for everyone: furniture, blankets, paint, over-the-counter drugs and cosmetics, car parts, building materials.

Nearly all clothing — at least the new store-bought variety, as opposed to hand-me-downs — was chosen from the catalog. Orders from Wards came mostly from Portland, although fashion items often came from the

Chicago warehouse — and we thought those would never come. Turnaround for orders filled in Portland was only about four days, all via mail. Whoever heard of phoning in an order? Sears' orders, filled in Seattle, took a little longer.

On the momentous day when the catalog came, the lucky one in our family who had gone to town that day to get the mail had first rights. But even when I was the one who proudly brought it home, Mother, the fair and impartial, did not permit me to monopolize that big volume for long. And almost everything in that catalog was of interest to us high-school girls, excluding spark plugs, tar paper and baby chicks.

Usually the most exciting offerings were at the front of the catalog: women's dresses, skirts, blouses, suits, coats, shoes, hose, undergarments. As I dreamed my way through those catalog dresses, glamorously draped on models — albeit bodies not exactly resembling mine — I liked everything I saw. Then I came to Page 35 and a beautiful pink cotton dress with puffed sleeves, full skirt and "fetching Peter Pan collar with contrasting bias trim." I fell madly in love with that dress.

I studied it in detail, then turned the page and forgot entirely about the pink dream-dress because there on Page 37 was the prettiest dress I'd ever seen: red and white printed rayon, two piece, white sailor collar, pleated skirt. Dance partners no doubt would swarm around me when I wore it to a dance.

Then came shoes to wear with those dresses, displayed on models with no trace of bunions or corns. Next came the hose. Mostly, one couldn't see the faces of the models, who possessed beautiful, long shapely legs, which were sheathed in rayon, silk or cotton, since those were pre-nylon days. And always the hose seams down the back of their legs were straight as a fence post. Next came the undergarments. The corsets did not interest me, but in those days before silicone implants, the undergarments gave one hope.

Few of those purchases actually materialized. The Montgomery Ward catalog was known as the wish book. And in addition to the big fall/winter, spring/summer catalogs, our friend tempted us with sale catalogs. The Christmas edition was pure delight. Kids ogled its vast toy collections: dolls, footballs, erector sets. Its pages were a fairyland of soft, warm robes, beguiling undergarments, cuddly slippers and candy and nuts.

I am sure Mother did not think I was discriminating when I studied the dresses in the catalog, Almost every dress merited an "Oh, I like that." "Oh, this is so cute." "Oh, look at that," or, "Oh, don't you think this would look good on me?"

Since almost everyone in Monument shopped via catalog, we often saw our wished-for clothing modeled by others. Sometimes, we then crossed it off our list, wondering why we'd liked it. But, if we thought it really spiffy, we might order it in a different color, hoping no one recognized it.

When we sent in an order, it was an important event. Mother sat at the kitchen table with pencil, newly sharpened by jack knife. The catalog number was carefully copied onto the order form, with color and size.

At one time, our good friends Wards and Sears paid postage on orders. That changed, and the customer paid, necessitating us to write on orders the weight of the ordered article. Postage cost then was inconsequential. Today shipping and handling charges on a single book, cost more than did a pair of shoes.

When the order arrived, the postmaster put a "Please call for package" notice in our box, and then at home there was the excitement of trying on the dress. It helped, of course, if one were a perfect size 10. If one seesawed between a size 12 and 14, it was difficult to decide whether to try to shuck a few pounds and go for the size 12 — or the 14 to give one breathing room. Sometimes the arrival signaled a sorry day — total disillusionment — as we saw how that dress looked on us compared to the way it looked on Page 37.

It was disappointing if Mother had forgotten to include a size or color on the order and a rubber stamp on the returned order advised, "Necessary information not supplied." Sometimes, too, we were advised: "Out of stock. Merchandise will be shipped in 10 days."

I miss those catalogs. They provided fine reading matter. I studied them by the hour.

And a husband, averse to shopping trips, must think of what a dandy era that would have been.

He then would never have had to go on a shopping trip with his wife.

CHAPTER 10

Every Morning, a Feast

Breakfasts at our eastern Oregon ranch were oversized affairs, not of the freshly squeezed orange juice and segmented grapefruit variety. They were cholesterol and calorie shockers.

In the morning, long before I was ousted from the featherbed, I heard preparations begin: coffee perking atop the wood-burning stove and my mother stirring the pancake batter in a big metal bowl, clacking the metal spoon against its side.

Sometimes the pancakes were sourdough — if Mother had remembered to provide for the starter — but whatever variety, pancakes were almost daily fare.

On the few mornings we did not have pancakes, we had sourdough or baking powder biscuits. There was no Bisquick on our kitchen shelf, and whatever the variety, biscuits were made without benefit of measuring cup or spoon.

They then went in a big black-tinned rectangular pan with biscuits snugged to the very edge. When you helped yourself to one of those biscuits, about as big as a saucer, you knew you had substance and not some dainty tea biscuit hardly big enough to break in two for butter.

On the rare mornings we did not have biscuits or pancakes, we had toast, made in the oven with some dozen slices arranged side-by-side and baked in that same black-tinned pan until they were crispy-dry and tan.

Had I been my Mother, I would have made toast every morning but she knew that pancakes were my stepfather's choice, with biscuits a second and toast running a poor third.

Mixing the batter was just the start of the pancake ritual. Having a good fire was most important. It had to be continually stoked to keep the heavy, long black griddle hot enough so that when a drop or two of water was dropped thereon it emitted the proper "spit." Then with spatula, a liberal quantity of lard was applied to the griddle. If the fire was not hot enough, the pancakes were unpalatably pale.

Mother took the first stint of baking while the rest of the family ate. The big griddle accommodated three luncheon-plate-sized pancakes, but that didn't keep up with us eaters, so she usually first accumulated a stack of baked pancakes so we would not have to wait. But after one or two from that mountain of pre-baked pancakes, we then began to wait for hot ones off the griddle.

When my sister or I finished, we took turns at baking so Mother could sit down. We knew our baking pretty well. When the bubbles began to pop on the unflipped pancakes, we knew it was then time to make the turn. We baked until the bowl of batter was gone. Pancakes not eaten by us humans were relished by our dogs.

Our syrup was not the store-bought Log Cabin kind. It, too, was made from scratch: sugar and water boiled together and flavored with Mapleine maple flavoring.

But pancakes were only a small part of our breakfasts. Always there was meat, hearty meat. Often it was venison. Our family favorite was venison heart or liver dredged in flour and fried in a black iron skillet, afloat in sizzling lard or bacon fat, until it was crackly on the outside.

Not just one or two pieces of meat per person, but a great platter of fried meat came to the table. Bacon sometimes was the breakfast fare, but not the thinly sliced kind that came in a see-through package. The rind was still attached to the big slab that Mother first had to slice. Those slices had backbone.

On mornings when we had fried meat for breakfast, Mother made a pan full of thick gravy in the pan in which she fried the meat. Our gravy was almost as thick as tapioca pudding. My stepfather liked it that way.

We didn't favor gravy that wouldn't stay put. If we had gravy it topped the pancakes and biscuits rather than syrup.

In another black iron skillet, Mother fried the eggs. Not just one egg apiece, but a whole platter of eggs if Mother's hens were laying. These eggs were not of the coddled type but eggs with "authority" that didn't jiggle when you slid them onto your plate.

But still, Mother's breakfasts did not end. We also had hot cereal. Not of the cunningly shaped, sugar-coated variety, but oatmeal, Cream of Wheat or cornmeal — a sizable potful. The Cream of Wheat was the only one of those three I could tolerate.

I hated that gray, pasty oatmeal, and, to this day, it is a dish I detest. I shall never forget my disappointment years later when six of us went to the Columbia Gorge Hotel for their acclaimed breakfast and the first thing they served, after fruit and juices, was a dish of their supposedly gourmet oatmeal.

We had the cornmeal less frequently than the other two hot cereals, and although Mother was a fine cook and valiantly tried to serve lumpless cornmeal mush, inevitably my dish of cornmeal had lumps. They did not want to go down. Occasionally, my throat pushed them back up.

Always, the sugar bowl was on the table and a liberal sprinkling of sugar topped the hot cereal. On good days, when the cows recently had calved, we had heavy, thick cream, manufactured by the separator.

We had no orange juice or fruit with breakfast and no daily paper to read. We had to collect our paper at the post office in Monument. The publication was delivered, the day after it was printed, by the U.S. mail. Nor did we have television or even turn on our battery radio to start the day. Consuming all that food was serious business. We settled down to eat, with conversation the only distraction.

These mornings, as I sit down at my breakfast of granola with skim milk and half an unsugared grapefruit, I think it no wonder that I do not get done what my mother did in her long, chore-packed day that then started after cooking that laborious breakfast.

Perhaps what I need to spur me to industry is a breakfast like Mother used to make.

CHAPTER 11

Ranchers Swore by Swearing

Many ranchers in eastern Oregon were prone to do a lot of swearing — and their swearing wasn't the kind done by Romeo and Juliet, who "swore" to love each other forever.

Eastern Oregon swearing was the "working" kind. Ranch life — and often not enough money — triggered such outbursts and mostly that swearing served a purpose.

Mark Twain was aware of the "soothing" power of swear and of its defusing benefit. He wrote, "When angry, count four; when very angry, swear." My stepfather, Lynn, swore a lot and mostly he didn't wait until he counted to four. His swearing might spew forth when he discovered of a morning that the water in the horse trough was frozen and the horses couldn't drink. Our temperamental binder that tied bundles with twine also brought forth a lot of swearing when it wouldn't properly tie. And Lynn's swearing could be heard all the way from the barn to the house if, when he was milking, a cow kicked over his bucket of milk.

It was mostly the ranchers on those eastern Oregon ranches who swore. For the most part, ranchers' wives didn't think it was ladylike — although ranch life gave them opportunities to use epithets.

Only rarely did my mother swear. When she did, her swearing vocabulary was a poor second to Lynn's — in part because she wasn't raised in eastern Oregon. Mother's swearing consisted of one word that replaced "darn" when "darn" wasn't forceful enough. But Mother put as much fervor in that one word as Lynn could in a whole mouthful. When she used that word, I didn't want to be the one who caused it.

We kids weren't supposed to swear. Nor did I find much reason to do so. Life was good. Life was fun. About my most stressful moment was when I went to bring in the cows and couldn't find them.

But boys — especially if they were the macho type and heard their dads swear — often thought it was manly to do so. If a boy swore, he was more apt to do so around his dad, since most mothers didn't countenance the therapy of swearing. Some dads seemingly enjoyed hearing their sons swear -- sort of "my son's growing up to be a man" kind of thing.

Assuredly, most people do not condone swearing, but in defense of the eastern Oregon ranchers' variety, their swearing was not the most offensive kind. Although it was blasphemous, it was not vulgar. Ranchers didn't use nasty four-letter words.

About the worst language that the ranchers brought forth, when something went very wrong, pertained to the heritage of the horse or cow or dog that was the cause of the swearing.

Ranchers did a lot of swearing because of animals, but inanimate objects needed to be sworn at as well. A gate that wouldn't fasten needed to be sworn at. A broken pipe that brought water from the spring to the house required swearing. A rusted plow bolt that couldn't be removed was another good reason to swear.

By no means did Lynn ever swear at my mother or us kids — even when I hiked up Rough Canyon and ran out all the deer when we were without venison and Lynn was planning to hunt up there — a sure place to find deer.

Lynn had other favorite things to swear at, including his saddle horse, Bug.

Bug was a big, black mean kind of horse, ridden only by Lynn. Bug objected to being saddled on frosty mornings, and when a horse doesn't stand still while one is trying to throw a saddle over his back, and hops and dances and shies, it's enough to make any rancher swear.

And when Lynn swore, I usually hustled far enough away to be out of ear-shot. Swearing was associated with something stressful, so it was just as well not to be around.

As a kid, I was always curious as to whether Bug knew he was being sworn at and if it helped shape him up. It didn't seem to me that Bug was much affected by the tirade. Rather, he needed to get all that energy and "acting up" out of his system, and then he'd permit the saddling.

A lot of ranchers we knew had sworn for so long they weren't even aware of using swear words in their normal conversation when there was no need to do so. They were "verbigerating" — a nice descriptive word that means repeating certain words or phrases unconsciously.

One day, our neighbor Slim, who was riding for cattle, stopped by and ate with us. He told Lynn he had found a cow that had been missing for a year. About every other word was a swear word — yet he must have been delighted to have found that cow.

I don't know anything about the origin of swearing, but I suspect it goes back forever and that even cavemen swore — or cursed. There's a slight line between cursing and swearing. A curse can be an invocation for harm or injury to come upon someone or something.

The last thing in the world that Lynn wanted to do was to bring injury or harm to Bug or one of his work horses, or his dog Binky. They were part of the work force. So perhaps on those frosty mornings when Bug did not want to be saddled, Lynn was swearing at the situation and not at Bug. At any rate, be was being careful not to impose a "curse."

Mark Twain probably had good advice with his suggestion to swear when one was very angry. It let one blow off steam — perhaps prevent an even more unpleasant happening.

Which prompts me to wonder. The next time I burn a batch of biscuits, if I resort to swearing, will it improve the biscuits or merely console me?

CHAPTER 12

Gates are Gold on a Ranch

Over in juniper and sagebrush country, leaving a gate open was about as serious a crime as rustling cattle.

And some of those gates were mighty hard to close.

Ranchers in those days didn't have elegant, initialed metal gates that open at the press of a button with secret codes.

Gates on our ranch, for the most part, were of the barbed wire variety: three rows of wire strung on wooden stakes. Whenever you tried to close a gate, the gate was at least a foot too short to reach. One's only reassurance was that it had been shut before, so seemingly it would agree to be closed again.

Each gate on our ranch had a different temperament — mostly a loath-some temperament — and a different best way to close it. With strange gates, it sometimes took a long time to figure out how to get them closed. With some, it worked better to put the stake in the top wire loop first; with others to put it in the bottom. Weaklings had a terrible time trying to snug the end post of the gate into those wire loops.

Some ranchers tied tin cans on their wire gates. I never knew why, unless it was to call attention to the gate so strangers wouldn't unknowingly drive through it. Sometimes gates didn't deter those strangers. They'd drive through on purpose. Or if we had a gate with a padlock, they might shoot their way through. Maybe the rattling cans helped, too, to dissuade breachy cattle from trying to get through a gate. Some of our breachy cattle were regular Houdinis. They could get through about any gate or fence if an alfalfa field was on the other side.

Gates, of course, were an annoyance to riders going through our ranch and drivers of vehicles going up the road through our ranch along the North Fork of the John Day.

But ranchers didn't just, on a whim, stick in a gate here and there. Those gates were just as unhandy for the owners.

Gates especially slowed down a rancher if he was traveling alone. If he was driving a vehicle, he'd get out, open the gate, get back in, drive through, get out, close the gate and then proceed down the road. If he was headed upriver with a team and load of hay, taking it to where cattle were to be wintered, when he came to a gate he had to crawl down from his perch on the wagon, open the gate, crawl back up in the wagon, drive the horses through, get back down, close the gate — all the while making sure his horses were under control so they didn't charge down the road while he was struggling with the gate.

If one were on foot — and somewhat athletic — it wasn't necessary to open the gate, although it helped if one had a companion who could hold the barbed wires apart when one crawled through. If one were alone and one's jacket or shirt caught on the upper strand while straddling the wire, it was extremely difficult to move backward or forward without sacrificing clothing — or skin.

Some gates on our ranch were the pole variety, and they were friendlier than the barbed wire type. An agile horseback rider could even open some pole gates without getting off his horse.

When my stepfather bought our uncleared section of land, it was unfenced. He then had to build four miles of fence to enclose our 640 acres. Next he must have done a lot of figuring by light of the coal oil lamp to determine where to put additional fences on his land, separating the cultivated areas from those not suitable for cultivation and used for grazing. Every parcel in which cattle were kept had to have water. A rancher had to have a good plan at the outset so he wouldn't build unnecessary fences. And more fences meant more gates.

Cattle guards, of course, were handy. The inventor of cattle guards was a clever man. But if you were driving a team or riding horseback, you still had to open gates. Our cattle guards were not the sleek, metal kind found on some state highways in northeastern Oregon that cars zoom over with scarcely a noticeable bump. Ours were made of wooden poles with spaces between. If a cow's hoof slid off one of those round poles when trying to cross a cattle guard, her leg would have been stuck between the poles. Cattle, in my estimation, were not a smart lot, but it was remarkable that they seemed to instinctively know that cattle guards were not for them. Never did we have a horse or cow imprisoned in cattle guard or treat one for a broken leg that tried to get across.

We worried a lot about gates being left open. An open gate allowed cattle to stray, requiring hours and hours — or days — of riding for them. And time was money to a rancher. Some gates were a considerable distance from the house and could be open without our knowing. Perhaps our first knowledge would be when the Nixons rang us up to tell us they'd seen a steer with our brand up in Ritter country.

If gates were left open, it could mean crop damage, too, and cattle could founder feeding on some of those crops.

Early on, every little kid in eastern Oregon learned the gate creed. If you find a gate closed, you close it. Likewise, a gate found open is left that way. Sometimes gates were left open purposely so cattle could get to water. If closed, those cattle were without water supply.

We didn't worry much about locals. They respected the gate creed. It was the visitors that we were concerned about.

As far as we knew, we never lost any cattle to rustlers and we had no "string 'em up" parties. But we fleetingly thought about staging a "string 'em up" party whenever a visitor left open a gate he found closed.

Monument to Service: Boyer's Cash Store

Although the little town of Monument was not incorporated and we had no mayor, we had a city hall. Boyer's Cash Grocery unofficially served in that capacity.

Boyer's was not just a grocery store, but a social oasis, bank, service station, department store, news dispenser and telephone office.

Other than a tavern-card room and a garage, it was about Monument's only business. In its heyday as a freighting center, Monument had a hotel and at one time two grocery stores. When its population dwindled down to some 125, two groceries could not be supported.

Ranchers in the area were largely self-sufficient and that cut down on grocery purchases. Ranch families had their own milk, eggs, chickens, pigs and beef, if they could afford to eat their cash crop. Ranchers' wives worked big gardens that supplied plenty of winter squash, onions, cabbage and potatoes — and fresh vegetables all summer.

The actual store building for Boyer's Cash Store was not super-market size. It was scarcely bigger than a home. Proprietor, Dempsey Boyer, his wife Nora, and children, Nona and Bub, lived in a home behind the store.

In front of the faded white, low-slung market were a couple of benches usually occupied by ranchers who had moved to town. A pair of locust trees provided shade. A nearby fence was handy for tying up the saddle horse if you rode to town. If your pickup needed gas, the pumps were in back and you went in the store's back door.

Tacked up outside the building on its walls and front door were important notices about coming events. The high school play, "Curse You, Jack Dalton," with dance following, was only two weeks hence. Jack Prosser was out a Hereford steer with the J-P brand, last seen up Wall Creek. Daisy Swenson had Rhode Island Red fryers to sell, and Dorothy Cooper was having a pink and blue shower for Mandy North on Tuesday. Everyone come. Here at Dempsey's, locals also learned about funerals since Monument had no newspaper, other than the Blue Mountain Eagle, published weekly in Canyon City, that contained Monument news.

Boyer's Cash Store, no doubt was so named by proprietor Dempsey Boyer in the hope that all transactions would be cash. He must have been mightily disappointed. The one cash crop for many ranchers was their cattle and they usually sold cattle only once a year.

Meanwhile, Dempsey carried their balance.

For each account of this non-cash type, Dempsey kept a little account book, hung by a string to a nail on the wall, like washing on a clothesline. When Mary Morrison, a rancher's wife, rode horseback to town to get a gallon of kerosene, Dempsey took down the little Morrison account book, reached for the stub pencil from behind his ear, wrote down date, purchase, and amount, adding it to the Morrison's running total.

Ranchers uneasily watched that total grow, with cash crop still months away. But Dempsey sent out no past-due notices. Nor did he add service charges or interest to those accounts.

Mother's chickens, when they laid more eggs than we could use, sometimes reduced our running total a bit. We traded eggs to Dempsey for lard, coffee, matches, sugar, and Dempsey sold the eggs to townspeople who didn't own chickens.

In addition, too, to all other entrepreneurial undertakings, Dempsey served as "central" for our phone system. When we, on the Mountain Line, wanted to call Capons, on the River Line, we called "Central" at Boyer's Store. Dempsey then put our call through to the River Line, ringing Capon's number.

For this service, Dempsey charged a nickel — that in time went up to a dime. But often in the press of his many other duties, he did not take the time to record that transaction in our account book,

Monument had no mayor, but we thought of Dempsey as filling that role. In dry, hot summer and fall, ranchers and townspeople alike feared fire and Monument had not a single piece of fire equipment. A motorist driving through — a stranger because all locals knew better — might toss out a cigarette and start a grass fire along the river road that could have burned up the entire township. When Leo Flowers shortly discovered the fire, he put through a call to Dempsey, whereupon Dempsey called ranchers for a local volunteer fire fighting unit.

Boyer's Cash Grocery served another purpose. It served as our social center. Even townspeople who ran in for a loaf of bread made it a social occasion.

While at the store, Betty White saw Irma Skinner and learned that Irma's daughter was expecting. Irma learned that Mrs. Sylvan was taken to Prairie City Hospital Friday and operated on for appendicitis. From Dempsey they learned that the strange car parked in front of the Johnsons' belonged to the Johnsons' married daughter, Carrie, up from Portland for a visit.

By the time you left Boyer's, you had been brought up to date on all happenings.

I lost track of happenings there in Monument after I left Monument to go to school and I do not know when Dempsey passed away. The store then was operated by Dempsey's son, Bub, in turn by Bub's son -- and then the next generation.

But I hope that at Dempsey's funeral he was properly eulogized — not only for his efforts to make Monument a better town, but because of the understanding and generosity extended ranchers who couldn't fill the bill as "Cash" customers during the Depression.

He, no doubt, was responsible for some of those local residents being able to stay on their land. Hopefully that is how the eulogists remembered him. Dempsey was a good man.

CHAPTER 14

Put It All on the Line

It's sad that Americans don't hang up clothes outdoors anymore and mostly toss them in the dryer instead.

It's therapeutic to hang clothes on the line. All's well when you're hanging up clothes — like picking a bouquet of flowers, reading a book, going for a walk. Hanging up clothes is a stress diffuser.

True, during rain-plagued Oregon winters a dryer is a godsend and I would not for the world give mine up. And on days when there is too much to do, dryers are wonderful. Toss in a load of washed clothes and it is easy to forget about them. Those dried clothes wait uncomplainingly in the dryer for days.

But on Oregon days when spring opens up like a flower and any excuse to get outside is a good one, then there should be a clothesline in every backyard.

Growing up before dryers were invented, my job as a grade-schooler was to hang up clothes. The long wire clotheslines at our eastern Oregon ranch bordered the garden and provided plenty of space.

Hanging up clothes required no thought, no knobs to turn, no buttons to twist, no worrying about whether the setting would be too hot for the rayon blouse and shrink it.

Although some tidy housewives grouped together on the line all similar clothes — as if towels, for example, were afraid of all other clothes — I, as an amateur clothesline hanger was not bothered with compulsive neatness. I cared not at all if a sock did not hang beside its mate.

Living on a ranch had advantages when hanging things on the line. No critical housewives lived near enough to eye our tea towels to see whether they were as snowy white as theirs. In town, one's personals were displayed on the line for all to see. Mrs. Smith notes that Mrs. Jones' husband wore only one pair of overalls for two weeks, that he changed shirts only twice. On a ranch, no one noticed if towels weren't as unblemished as a clean sheet of paper, or if there was an occasional rent in a bed sheet.

Hanging up clothes in the winter was not quite as joyful as doing it on a nice summer day.

Monday was designated wash day, but Mother checked the weather first. If it was raining, wash day was postponed until, in time, we might almost be out of clean clothes. On clear winter days, even on the coldest, the washing would proceed. The wet clothes froze almost as soon as the clothespins affixed them to the line. The tea towels quickly stiffened into boards and my stepfather's union suit, frozen stiff, jumped about in the wind as if doing a dance. By the time the clothes were hung, my hands burned from the cold.

But on days when the sun aired the clothes and the breeze blew them about, the sheets had a fresh-air smell. The sun and the wind seemed to renew the garments. And there was a nice sense of satisfaction in folding the sun-warmed cloth.

In our early married days, before I had a dryer, I had no outdoor clothesline. Hanging clothes on a line in the garage is not nearly as satisfactory as hanging them outside.

It was particularly unsatisfactory at the time because we had a lively red setter and when Homer and I were at work, Red was unhappy at being left alone. He entertained himself by jumping up — and he could jump as high as an Olympic medalist — and pulling clothes from the line.

I had Homer raise the clothesline in the garage, but Red accepted it as a challenge. He destroyed a good many of our clothes. When we bought a dryer, our clothes replacement cost went down considerably.

True, before dryers became commonplace, families with babies had a bad time. It was difficult to get cloth diapers to dry outside in damp weather. Some distraught homemakers turned to indoor dryers — little wooden racks one put behind the stove. When the diapers steamed next to the hot stove, the room was like a sauna. And in one's eagerness to get clothes dry, one had to be careful to not get them so close to the stove that they scorched.

Believe me, I do not want to give up my dryer. If one is in a hurry, throwing in a load of wash, turning a knob, and a bit later taking out dry clothes, is a great boon. It's a godsend, too, when one does not for days see the sun.

But on warm summer days, I still hang clothes outside. It lets one see the beautiful morning. It requires no thought. A little breeze tumbles the clothes, and in the evening I go to retrieve them and they have a fresh-air smell not present on clothes from the dryer. The towels are not as soft as when dried in the machine, but they seem almost more purposeful if line dried. I use them after my shower and they wake up my skin.

I'm sorry to see outdoor clotheslines disappear. The best of both worlds is to have a dryer — and an outdoor clothesline too.

That clothesline on our ranch knew a lot of my secrets.

CHAPTER 15

Venison in the Feather Bed

On our eastern Oregon ranch in the 1930s, we had no valuables under our mattress — but we sometimes had illegally killed venison in our feather bed.

Even when we raised cattle, no beef came to our table. It was our cash crop.

Instead, venison was the year around fare. Deer-hunting was a necessity and Lynn kept our family well supplied.

We often had venison three meals a day. Breakfast was venison steak, eggs, sourdough biscuits or pancakes and gravy. Fried venison steak for dinner. Venison again for supper. We were meat and potato eaters, bolstered by a garden during summer.

When Mother announced to Lynn that our venison supply was running low, he took down from the kitchen wall his battered .30/.30 lever-action Savage, with taped and wired stock and canted front sight, and went hunting. Often an hour's horseback ride to the pasture sufficed. Daniel Boone wasn't a better hunter or shot.

Some horses were afraid of a dead deer and would not carry one back to the house in the saddle. If Lynn chanced to be riding such a horse when he shot and killed a deer, he then came back to the ranch house to get Bubbles, our combination saddle-work horse that he didn't deign to ride.

Mother, seeing him walking toward the house empty handed, would think disappointedly that he had had no luck until we saw the blood stains on his hands— evidence of dressing out the deer. Our Blue Mountains had few springs or streams where he could wash off that sure giveaway.

When Lynn rode his saddle horse, Bug, there was no doubt we had fresh meat. We'd spot Lynn walking down the, trail with the deer thrown across Bug's saddle, stirrups tied up to hold the kill. Mother met him at the barn, untying from the back of the saddle the flour sack that contained liver and heart.

At the house, the deer was hoisted with heavy rope to hang from a beam on the porch. A stick of kindling wedged horizontally in the rib cage enabled it to cool more quickly and made it rigid and easier to skin.

During the ceremonial skinning, dogs and cats gathered around awaiting morsels of trimming or fat — until the boss dog perhaps drove the others away.

Then I had the task of taking the cut-off head over into the little canyon to cache midst sagebrush and junipers. That kept it from littering the yard and removed evidence, if unfriendly visitors came to call

After soaking in cold, salted water, liver and heart were eaten at the next meal. The meat was sliced thin, liberally floured. A plentiful quantity of lard in the cast iron skillet sputtered and popped. No one worried about cholesterol. The meat was browned well on both sides, cooked until crispy and well done.

Hams, a choice part of the deer, usually became steaks — sliced thin and fried, cooked well. Venison never came to our table rare. Sometimes for us five, two big skillets of steaks sizzled away. Ribs were used last and weren't much to our liking.

Lacking refrigeration, venison usually hung on the back porch in a wool sack or flour sacks. During the winter this served well except when mother tried to cut the frozen meat.

In summer it was a different matter. When the still-searing sun caught the back porch in late afternoon the meat was moved to the shade of the woodshed. Come evening after flies no longer buzzed, the protective flour sacks were removed so cool air circulated about the meat.

Those flies were the deadliest scourge of our fresh meat supply. If the offensive steel-blue blowflies could get to that venison, they laid eggs thereon. We called it "blowing" the meat. That meant the supply was chucked out, given to the dogs.

Despite lack of refrigeration, scant meat spoiled — perhaps because we ate it three times a day. And no part of that deer went to waste. Even the exterior of the meat, which became hard and glazed with exposure to air, was food for the dogs. Dog food was never bought.

When Mother took down a ham from its nail on the porch, the dogs hunkered at her elbow until trimming was done. She was careful to give our working dogs equal amounts, but for Major and her two little pop-eyed Pekingese that she later acquired, it was different. Although they served no purpose on a cattle ranch except for love we bestowed on them, special tender little morsels were secreted to them.

Sometimes during haying or plowing if we ran out of meat, and Lynn would be unable to take time to hunt, Mother was hard put to provide a meal that pleased.

Then she resorted to beans and salt pork, perhaps macaroni and cheese or sheepherder potatoes that Mother had never heard of before coming to eastern Oregon. Salt pork and onion were browned in a big skillet, covered with peeled, sliced raw potatoes, salt and pepper, covered with boiling water, and simmered, with lid, until mushy and well done.

It was not just that there was no money for meat. Wieners, and occasionally hamburger, were about the only choices at Boyer's Cash Grocery.

Although we had little chance to compare, we thought we would have been hard pressed to tell our venison from beef. In large measure, we attributed that to Lynn's considerable experience in dressing and taking care of venison.

If the deer was killed on a side hill, he was careful its head was lower than the rest of the body so it bled properly.

He regarded it as amateurish if bladder or intestines were slit during the dressing, and got on the meat. During skinning he was careful to keep the deer hair away from the meat. He said hair gave venison an unpleasant taste. Before cooking, all fat was trimmed from the meat. Lynn said that tallow sometimes gave the meat a gamey taste.

But, as an experienced hunter, the first thing Lynn always did after shooting a deer was to cut the animal's throat — not only to bleed the deer but to make certain it was dead. More than one old-timer had had a scary experience when a "dead" deer came to life.

During hunting season, when we saw deer hauled back to the city, still not skinned, baking in the sun atop a car without protection from dust and flies, we thought it no wonder many city people did not like venison.

Only rarely did we get a deer that was off-flavor. A bad omen was if the neck of a buck was swelled — a sign of rutting season.

We were not alone in our use of venison year-round. Neighboring ranchers did likewise. If a rancher friend's venison supply ran low, we might loan him a ham until that rancher could take time to go hunting.

But we did not abuse our resource. If Lynn wounded a deer, he spent hours tracking it down — with the dogs' help. It was a mean hunter who left a wounded animal to suffer, or let its meat go to waste.

Perhaps because Mother was not raised in eastern Oregon, this illegal venison, killed out of season, worried her no end. Whenever a stranger's car approached, she worried that it might be a game warden or that someone who knew we had venison out of season had "squealed."

So Mother viewed no approaching visitor as friendly. Most visitors entered by the back porch where venison often hung, so she had to quickly hide it away. Usually she hid it in the feather bed, the heavy carcass sinking in so that when it was covered with quilts there was scarcely a sign.

Although headquarters for State Police was some 60 miles away in John Day, when a game warden was transferred to our territory, his reputation usually preceded him. If he was a known son-of-a-gun, Mother was even more eagle-eyed watching the turnoff to our road. We were never caught with venison out of season but I suspect we fooled those wardens not one bit.

They knew we didn't kill deer for sport, didn't kill doe that had fawn, didn't waste meat. And the deer deprived our cattle of grass, ate our alfalfa, eroded our hay stacks.

Venison was a necessity for cattle ranchers during the Depression — a necessity we were not about to abuse.

CHAPTER 16

Where There's a Quill…

When we moved to eastern Oregon when I was 8 years old, I was much in awe of porcupines and feared them more than rattlesnakes. I thought porcupines could throw their quills.

When I hiked the hills on our ranch, I thought how terrible it would be, if I suddenly was shot — pow! — by a porcupine quill in a vulnerable spot.

My stepfather who was raised in eastern Oregon relieved my fears. "They can't throw their quills," he said. But still I thought those big black and gray rodents with the armor of quills were the strangest animals I'd ever seen.

So did our dogs. They couldn't leave them alone. Though intelligent, our pets didn't learn from previous encounters. Apparently they thought porcupines were mortal enemies, and after living on the ranch for a while I understood why. Although the dogs usually were bigger, more agile, and had sharp teeth, I never saw a dog who won a fight with a porcupine. Instead, the dogs came whimpering home with quills imbedded in their face — particularly in the soft fleshy area around the nose — and then a terrible operation would take place.

Our "experienced" dogs know how dreadful this removal was, and if they had had previous encounters with porcupines and lost, they'd come slinking home, wondering if it wouldn't be better to live out in the wild with a face full of quills rather than to face removal.

My stepfather would fetch a pair of pliers and firmly holding down the terrified dog, pull the quills from its nose.

No veterinarians were available and even had they been we could not have afforded them. So the poor dogs suffered terribly having quills removed. They didn't come out smoothly like a sliver. Rather, they had a little barb on the imbedded end, like a fishhook.

Along with the unfounded theory that porcupines could throw quills, there was a belief that if they were left in the flesh, the quills continued to burrow in — deeper and deeper.

My stepfather showed me the intricacies of quills one day when a big porcupine ambled across the road. He got a board and stuck it out toward the porcupine's big tail and it flopped around at will. The porcupine left several of his quills in the board. I gathered up those little black and white hollow stilettos and kept them among my treasures.

Actually we eastern Oregonians were never sure how porcupines fit into the scheme of things and what they did for the good of the cause. We were very aware of the damage they did — such as harvesting our fruit. Usually they got more than we.

Ranchers had a trick that helped keep porcupines out of fruit trees. They nailed a smooth sheet of metal around the tree trunk several feet off the ground. Porcupines couldn't clamber over this slick surface.

I never had a porcupine quill imbedded in any part of my body, nor did anyone I knew, but on one occasion a porcupine gave me a real start. After my stepfather passed away and the old ranch house was deserted, my sister, her husband, their children and I would go up and camp for a week at the old house. My Mother enjoyed going too. She opted to sleep inside the old ranch house, while I, suspecting it now was occupied by packrats and bats, would have slept anywhere else. I set up my cot on the porch of the house. The porch had a roof and a wall at one end that extended out from the house and offered shelter from the wind.

One night as I slept fitfully in my sleeping bag, I heard a strange shuffling sound — as if something were being dragged along on the old dry porch boards. It sounded as if it were big. I reached for my flashlight and there, waddling across the porch and about to go into the house where

Mother was sleeping near the door, was a big porcupine. In the light of the flashlight it looked enormous.

I couldn't let it go into the house. I was afraid it would frighten Mother if she chanced to wake up, and for all I knew regarding the ways of porcupines, it might even crawl up on the cot where she slept.

I scooted from my sleeping bag and in bare feet beat the porcupine to the door of the house and shooed him away from the door. I thought he would be frightened of a human at such close quarters and that he would hurry away into the night. Instead, he headed for the corner of the porch. Then, with head in the corner and lethal weapon of a tail pointing out at me, he mounted his defense.

I tried to scare him out of the corner. I waved my arms. My flashlight wasn't long enough to use as a prod. I stamped my bare feet and focused the beam of light on his head. He did not budge. Finally, I scouted around the dark yard and found a long piece of tree limb so I could reach in and pry him from his lair.

Fearful that he might return, I stayed awake to make sure he didn't come back and crawl up on one of our cots. It wasn't quills that the porcupine "shot" that night.

He shot down my night's sleep.

CHAPTER 17

Down in the Scary Dark Cellar

Had I known about boogiemen when I was a kid, I would have expected then to be in our cellar.

Most eastern Oregon ranches had cellars. We had no other refrigeration and had not yet known the glory of a kerosene refrigerator. In the winter, cellars protected our food from freezing.

Unlike the cellars at some ranches, ours was utilitarian and "bare bones" with dirt walls, dirt steps and dirt floor. It had few amenities except for wooden shelves around the upper portion and bins on the floor. It was dark and scary.

This was the storage place for Mother's canned fruit, pickles, apple butter, chokecherry jelly — and dozens of quarts of canned tomatoes. Canned tomatoes were big at our house in the winter.

Along with those jars of canned goods, our winter vegetables: squash, potatoes, onions — were stored underground.

Mother never took our pans and buckets of milk and cream to the cellar. Those containers were covered only with flour-sack dishtowels which would have offered slight discouragement to any crawling creatures that lurked in the cavern.

Usually our milk supply, replaced with twice-daily milkings, stayed sweet without refrigeration. In the summer, when temperatures soared above 100 degrees, the milk never had a chance to cool down before the heat of the day. It occasionally soured, complicating Mother's cooking no end.

We believed that thunderstorms always soured milk. If we heard the rumble of thunder off in the Blue Mountains, Mother would comment that now she'd have no milk to use for making supper.

Our cellar served another purpose in addition to refrigeration and storage. When we had high windstorms, Mother sought protection there. I felt safer above ground. Luckily, no tornadoes made sanctuary in that cellar mandatory.

The only thing that I liked about cellars was the story my Mother told about her experiences as a little girl. Her mother passed away when she was young and my grandfather, who worked on the railroad, hired a Chinese cook and housekeeper. Whenever the cook went down into the cellar, my Mother and her several young brothers slammed the cellar door shut and sat on it so he could not get out. He found an answer for their impudence. He started carrying a long butcher knife whenever he went to the cellar, ostensibly to cut off a piece of squash or for some other purpose. When these impish youngsters climbed onto the door, he ran his butcher knife up through the cracks. Mother and her brothers took great delight in trying to stay on the door — while avoiding the butcher knife as it sliced through the cracks.

We had no cook and there was nothing entertaining about our cellar. When Mother asked me to get a jar of applesauce or an onion, I regarded it as major trauma.

In the dark, as I reached in the bin for an onion, I had horrors of touching something furry, which might attack and perhaps dispose of me before Mother knew I was imperiled. I reasoned that surely the protective darkness of that cellar was the perfect home for any knowing animal, snake or insect.

Although I could have lit the kerosene lantern and taken it to light up the dark corners, I was ashamed to let Mother know that I was afraid.

Never did I see any living creatures in my hurried trips down to the cellar.

Never did I see boogiemen. Nevertheless, I am sure they were there — over in that darkest corner.

CHAPTER 18

Memories of Remedies

Our town, Monument, had no doctor or dentist when I was growing up. But every mom had prescriptions, some handed down for generations. In some cases, I preferred to be ill.

Our nearest doctor was in John Day, about 60 miles, although occasionally a doctor settled briefly in Long Creek, some 25 miles distant. My younger sister was born in a Long Creek doctor's "hospital" that was in his home.

Only once did I go to a doctor when I was a child. At age 6, before moving to eastern Oregon, I underwent routine removal of adenoids and tonsils by Dr. Bilderback in Portland, a surgery performed on just about all little boys and girls in those days.

Lacking doctors in Monument, I was "doctored" by Mother. At first sign of chest cold or cough, she brought forth turpentine and lard to liberally smear on my chest. A woolen cloth was placed over all and safety-pinned to pajamas to keep it in place.

The wool cloth scratched. The fumes oozed into my eyes and nose from underneath the cloth. The lard was slick and greasy. I vowed I would be well by morning.

In time, this treatment was replaced by Mentholatum or Vicks Vapo-Rub. Although I could not speak as to whether they were a more reliable cure, they offered only slight improvement. Their fumes still wafted into nose and eyes. The wool cloth still scratched.

Liniment was another of Mother's medicinal standbys: great for rheumatism, muscular aches and pains. Sometimes, it was called horse liniment, although I do not recall that we used it on a horse. And always, a bottle of Mercurochrome or iodine was at the ready, a favorite for cuts. My favorite disinfectant was hydrogen peroxide. Mother explained that the tiny bubbles that formed when it was applied to an open wound indicated that the peroxide was working — the more bubbles, the more germs.

But others of Mother's reliables were terrible: cod-liver oil, castor oil and/or Castoria. Each day, she poured out tablespoons of greasy, vile tasting, vomit-inducing cod-liver oil, apparently then a universal prescription for all youngsters. My husband Homer's daily dosage, he said, was mixed with grape juice to disguise the awful taste. To this day, he dislikes grape juice.

Castoria, or castor oil, a laxative as I recall, at least was not administered daily. I made sure of that. But Homer's mother, on the other hand, believed all children should be purged clean, twice annually with a massive dose of castor oil, whether needed or not.

We had another remedy: a bottle of whiskey, strictly for medicinal purposes, although perhaps some adults didn't mind getting a cold. A hot toddy seemed to work miracles.

Whiskey was good for animals, as well. When a newly born lamb was found almost frozen to death as Lynn made his early morning rounds during lambing, the inert little lamb was brought to the house, placed on a gunny sack on the open oven door of the kitchen stove and whiskey was forced down its throat. Usually within minutes, the little lamb began kicking and coming back to life.

We did not go to great lengths to avoid exposure to communicable diseases such as chicken pox and measles. Some mothers thought it best for a child to get those out of the way at an early age. In Monument, when one resident came down with something communicable, those diseases pretty much made the rounds. But before moving to eastern Oregon, when I had a light case of scarlet fever (then called "scarlet tina"), I was mortified when authorities tacked a sign on our door advising all comers that a person with a communicable disease was within.

Nor did we in eastern Oregon regularly go to dentists, although our water was perhaps responsible for good teeth. I did not visit a dentist until I was in college. In Monument, the prescription was not dentists but rather oil of cloves or a whole clove clamped down, on an aching tooth. Some of those old-time remedies perhaps had considerable merit. When Homer was bothered with ulcers, his grandmother, then nearly 100, told him to eat sauerkraut. Homer and I, of a modern generation, smiled knowingly at each other. Years later, we read that sauerkraut indeed was presumably helpful for such.

Today, our medics successfully treat maladies that in earlier days were not even known to exist, such as appendicitis. One of my uncles died of a ruptured appendix. We learned that in pioneer days, what doctors often diagnosed as inflammation of the bowel or of the stomach perhaps was appendicitis. Nowadays, we make appointments for annual check-ups months in advance to assure that we do not forget. We undergo procedures and annual tests on our blood, X-rays, mammograms, smears of this and that — all of which is wonderfully preventive.

Compared to last century's almost bare medicine cabinets, ours today are crammed with little pills taken daily to ward off osteoporosis, hormone pills to aid mature women, vitamin pills containing zinc to possibly guard against retina damage, Vitamin E tablets although I am not certain what they are for, all-around vitamin pills designed to provide alertness and vigor. Even our cosmetics contain "renewal" factors and sunscreen.

But we owe thanks to more than miracles of modern medicine for our health these days. Surely, we must give thanks to our sturdy forebears. Is it not surprising that they lived as long as they did?

CHAPTER 19

Old George: One Smart Dog

Although some contend that animals can't think, our sheepdog, Old George, could out think his owners. He was one smart dog.

He arrived at our eastern Oregon ranch as the gift of a neighbor. The neighbor, no doubt, had an oversupply of dogs at that time. He insisted that George was a fine worker and an intelligent one.

We needed a good sheepdog, so we adopted Old George, a medium-sized black and white shaggy creature with sad, pleading eyes. His parentage was unknown.

We were delighted after we tried him that first night. George was sent to hurry along the cows that were feeding halfway up the hill behind the house. We patted him a few times, waved an arm at the cows.

"Go get 'em, George," we commanded. George took off like a shot. Straight up the mountain he charged toward the startled cows. "Bring 'em down, George," we hallooed, and George barked acquiescence. Down the hill waddled the protesting cows, udders swishing wildly. In no time they were at the corral gate.

"Come on back, George," we called. "Good dog. Good dog." George strutted into the yard as erect as an old soldier. "Fine feller," we chorused, gathering around him. We had found ourselves a good dog.

But as time went on, George, we found, had a fault. He was intelligent but ambition he did not have. As George became a fixture, that analysis changed. George was just plain lazy. That trait was most pronounced on hot summer days.

We had a small band of sheep and George was our only sheep dog. He could have been of considerable assistance — and our cash supply during that Depression did not permit us to hire human help. Instead of being a helper however, he often was the recipient of the roughest language ever directed toward a cur. We became concerned as to whether George's age could be affecting his hearing and eyesight.

Our sheep — our one cash crop at that time — were pastured in a half-section that was mostly up and down. At the bottom of a vast mountain, topped with rims, suddenly would appear a small group of sheep rapidly headed away from the others.

If George did his job, after pointing in that general direction and shouting "Bring 'em back, George," the chastened wanderers shortly would be back with the herd. Such, we soon noted, began not to be the case.

We would point out the strays to George, but evidently we weren't making our wishes clear. He would disappear and that would be the last we'd see of him. We assumed George was combing the mountain for strays.

George's undoing came on one of summer's hottest days. Far up the mountain, we spied a few sheep headed in the wrong direction, away from the rest of the herd. I patted Old George and decided to again try to explain what was expected of him. I knelt beside him, pleadingly. It was far too hot to climb that mountain. I begged him to see those sheep — that little bunch on top of that hill so far away — that really wouldn't take a fine dog like George long to reach.

He started out confidently. I heaved a sigh and sat down to wait while the dog did the work.

George, however, had again confused his signals. There was no sign of him and that errant band of sheep was getting even farther away. It was up to me to bring them back. Reluctantly, perspiration trickling down forehead, I started up the mountain by a circuitous route to take advantage of the few shade trees and a more gentle incline.

I had climbed about a hundred yards when I heard an odd noise — a panting, slobbering sound. I held my own heaving breaths to better hear. The sound came from behind a mahogany with growth too thick to see through. I crept around it.

There, to my astonishment was George — sprawled out and lolling in the shade, and if ever a dog looked pleased with himself it was he. He was grinning with happiness as he rested in his hiding place.

"George," I screamed and I'm sure he'll remember that scream in the afterworld. He leaped to his feet and looked at me pleadingly. "Get up that hill, you dog, and don't come back till you bring down those sheep."

George obediently started up the hill. The strays were soon back with the herd. We thought surely that catching him in the act would cure George of his lazy habit, but shame he seemed not to know. From that day we knew our directions were plain to George. It was the steepness of the hill, the temperature, and his own feeling about the world that determined whether he would go willingly — or trot out of sight and lie down in the cool shade.

Some say that animals are not "thinkers" — but Old George was a thinking dog who could out think his owners.

CHAPTER 20

The Lost Art of Tracking Bee Trees

Whether it was huckleberries from the high mountains or venison out of season, it was customary in eastern Oregon to take what the land could give when times were hard in the 1930s.

Keeping the honey jar filled wasn't as easy for ranchers as procuring the huckleberries or venison. A rancher first had to find a bee tree — but sometimes he got lucky.

Sometimes, as a rancher rode down a trail he'd ridden just a few days before, he'd come to a gnarled old landmark of a hollow tree and clumped around the mouth of that opening was a big cluster of bees. That rancher had found himself a bee tree.

Ranchers knew their land well. As they rode for cattle, brought in the cows, or went out to catch a horse in the pasture, they noted anything new — all signs of wildlife.

Eastern Oregon ranchers were skilled at tracking everything — a wounded deer, cattle they were riding for, an uninvited coyote — and some ranchers could track down bee trees.

As they rode the trail they might happen to note a steady flight of bees headed toward West Gulch or Johnny Cake Mountain — and if they had the time and were hungry for honey, they might try to follow those bees in their flight.

The bees might not always lead that rancher to a bee tree on his first try. He might follow them a quarter of a mile — then pick up another flight of bees if he lost the first. And sometimes he might pick up the trail the next day, or even the next week — and then come upon the bee tree.

Ranchers weren't nearly as adept around bees as they were around horses and cattle. Few, if any of those ranchers kept hives or knew how to professionally handle bees. But when a rancher rode by and spotted that bee tree, the thought of melted honey on a hot sourdough biscuit was enough for him to take on a new experience. If he'd never robbed a bee tree, he could call a neighboring rancher who had experience extricating honey and learn the best way to proceed without getting stung. Or he might persuade him to come along and they'd go halfers.

Ranchers' wives stitched up devices for covering the head and hands. Sulfur was used to smoke out the bees, and hopefully render them inert. Then, from the hollow in that tree, the ranchers removed the honey in the comb and placed it in a wash tub for the trip home.

I never attended a bee-tree robbing but I remember the results.

After the wash tub was delivered to the house, the rancher's wife melted down the comb, separating the honey from the wax. If she didn't immediately get around to that task, some of the honeycomb might come to the table as it came from the tree.

Today the honey you buy is designated by flavor, such as clover. I wondered about the flavor of that honey we had from bee trees. Our ranch was dry-land farming, so the honey would not have been clover or alfalfa unless the bees went afar. Probably it was mahogany or sagebrush since we had an abundance of that, but we weren't interested in the particular flavor of our honey. Whatever it was, most ranchers thought it quite good.

I liked the honey well enough when it wasn't mixed with the wax, but the bee bread was most unpalatable when it was in the finished product. It's been a long time since I've heard of a rancher robbing a bee tree. Maybe there aren't any bee trees out there anymore.

Hopefully, that plundering of those trees did not result in the demise of the bee in that part of the country, although it surely must have been discouraging for the bees when a rancher came along and stole their food.

During the Depression, an eastern Oregon rancher didn't expect to find a gold mine or an oil well on his ranch but finding a bee tree was at least a small coup.

CHAPTER 21

Lord (or Lady) of the Flies

Late summer every year, they swarmed into our ranch house in eastern Oregon: the invasion of the houseflies. Screens on windows and doors were a luxury that most ranch houses did not have, so we coped with them as best we could.

My Mother, who had not experienced an invasion of this sort before moving to the ranch, detested those pesky creatures. The encyclopedia notes that there are 75,000 different kinds of flies, and she hated every one.

Ranch wives dealt with the flies in different ways. Some swore by flypaper. Festooned about kitchens all over eastern Oregon were coiled devices, about three feet long and an inch wide that dangled from the ceiling. The paper, covered with a sticky substance, was formulated to be the death of flies. Once a fly lit on that surface, it stuck there for the rest of its life, and at that point, no doubt, the fly hoped it would be short-lived. It was not pleasant to look at those flypapers dotted with flies all wiggling to extricate themselves.

These flycatchers hung from the ceiling until the housewife decided there was no longer surface on which more flies could light, She then burned them in the kitchen stove and up went a fresh one.

Another type of fly paper product was available but it was less popular.

It was a rectangle of sticky-surfaced paper that did not hang from the ceiling but was strategically placed around the house. Their disadvantage was that kids, pets and adults always were getting stuck on them, too.

Much as Mother disliked flies, she did not approve of either of these fly paper products. And even if one used those products, it seemed a useless battle, especially in late summer.

"My, the flies are dreadful today," she would say and I knew then what was next.

At least once a day, sometimes more often, she assigned me the task of swatting flies for 15 minutes or a half hour. With flyswatter in hand, I stalked the creatures, watching the clock all the while. There was no shortage of flies, but there were designated places where one did not make the kill, such as near the cake that Mother was stirring up or around the open pan of gravy on the stove, although mostly, Mother covered all kettles into which a fly could drop, or which a brazen fly might try to sample. Food, if not on the stove, was draped with a dish towel to keep out flies.

Sometimes I tried to keep track of my kills and set a new record, but this became tiresome after the first few minutes. Killing flies was not a challenging task, thereby permitting one to think about things other than being executioner. So I daydreamed about writing best-selling books, about new clothes that would complement my wardrobe come fall or about castles in Spain that did not have flies.

The most distasteful part of the job was that, in addition to killing the flies, Mother insisted on disposal thereof. She did not tolerate dead fly bodies left around, so I removed them as they were killed. Perhaps my killing alleviated the fly population somewhat, but to me it seemed quite useless. A new migration of flies immediately moved in to replace those killed.

Even after I served a stint at killing flies, busy though Mother was, she would pick up the flyswatter between mixing up the cake and browning a roast, and go after them. She cared nothing about endangering the species. Her goal was to eliminate every fly on Earth — particularly those that came into her kitchen.

I disliked the flies for a different reason. In late summer, they interrupted one's reading. Deep in a mystery at the most exciting part, a fly would choose me as its target, lighting perhaps first on my arm. Almost unconsciously, I brushed him away at first. But the fly, not to be discouraged, was back in a few seconds, sticking and crawling on any bare skin.

After a third or fourth time of waving him away, one realized this is no ordinary fly but one with a personal vendetta against you. It distracted one from reading to fight flies all the time.

Eastern Oregon restaurants had to cope with flies, too. Some had devices that used the electric chair approach but hung from the ceiling so as not to involve customers. When a fly lighted on this device, even if one were not watching the execution, it could be heard. The fly made a little "pop" when it landed on the fly killer and was instantly electrocuted.

Nowadays, despite being protected by screens, these invading flies are a pesky annoyance. Like a Daniel Boone, I track a sole fly about the house, flyswatter in hand. I first note it in the corner of the window, but use an indirect stroke so as not to break the glass. I miss it. It is a wary creature. Next it lights on a vase, one it knows I particularly like, so I cannot swat at him for fear I will break it. I wait for the fly to light on a flat surface but now it disappears. I wander about trying to find it, knowing that flies are short-lived, and hope that it has passed on. I put the swatter away and out it comes again.

About the only good thing about houseflies is that they don't bite, whereas the horseflies that bugged our horses in the summer bit not just the horses but inflicted painful bites when they settled on us humans.

Nature was the only one who knew how to deal with the housefly. Those flies pestered us all summer, sticking and crawling and dropping in the kettle of applesauce. But finally, Nature stepped in and the next morning at our ranch, we'd wake up to a heavy frost. Mother was one happy lady that morning. She held no wake for the passing of the flies.

CHAPTER 22

Stacks of Warm Memories

The size of a cattle herd and the number of haystacks weren't the only things that determined a wife's happiness on an eastern Oregon ranch. In decades past, the size of a woodpile also had much to do with marital relationships.

Before electricity came to ranches, wood was used for cooking and heating, and husbands were largely responsible for making certain a supply of wood always was on hand.

My Mother wasn't often grumpy, but if she ran out of chopped wood, it was a bad day for us all. Chopping wood was as much a daily chore of husbands as cooking three daily meals was for the wives. After working all day in the fields, plus feeding and watering the horses, milking the cows and countless other chores, husbands still faced the job of chopping the day's wood supply.

Wood did not arrive in a truck and magically become neatly stacked cords — but the price of our wood supply was right.

All year long on our 640 acres, my stepfather, Lynn, kept an eye out for fallen trees as a source for our wood supply. Late fall, after haying, plowing, disking and seeding, he harvested the year's wood.

The fallen trees that were cut up and hauled back to the ranch house with team and wagon often weren't even near our dirt roads. Wet weather and snow might make it impossible to get the hauling job done.

And, in addition to the hauling, every evening, after Lynn came in from the fields, he had to chop enough wood to last for the next 24 hours. In cold weather our heating stove -- plus cookstove -- used a tremendous amount.

Limbs made up much of our wood supply, and they at least required less chopping than the trunk of a tree. We couldn't afford a wood saw. Lynn tackled the job with an axe.

Making kindling was part of the wood chopper's job. That helped to assure that the fire in the morning would readily start. Each morning, warm in my bed, I awakened to the sound of paper being wadded up and placed in the firebox along with kindling and wood. Sometimes, after Lynn started the fire, he went back to bed while the house warmed. It was not a good day, if the fire went out.

After the wood was chopped each evening, my job was to bring in enough for the night. After each load, I inquired if that was enough. And with each load I was reminded by Mother to not dump my armful of wood against the wallpaper behind the wood heater. Mother put up with having the wood piled inside only so someone wouldn't have to go out to the woodpile at night every time the stove needed replenishment.

For a ranch wife, not only a sufficient supply of wood, but the size of the chopped wood for the kitchen stove, did much to determine her mood.

If one couldn't get a fire to burn, it was hard to brown the biscuits. If the wood was too long and the stove door had to be left ajar with the wood sticking out, not only did it make cooking difficult but one needed a smoke mask.

If the wood was too big, it not only was hard to cram into the fire box but it did not burn well. And even conscientious wood choppers had a tendency to leave the wood as big as possible to avoid unnecessary chopping. Then, too, if the wood was too small, it burned too fast.

If Lynn underestimated and chopped too little wood, it was an unpleasant day. Mother was not a good wood chopper. She couldn't get the axe to come down twice in the same place. I thought it would be fun to try to wield that axe but Mother thought I was too little and might cut off a foot.

As summer came on, the size of our year's wood supply was anxiously watched for fear we'd run out before Lynn finished spring planting, and harvesting.

Although a fire in the heater became unnecessary as summer arrived, wood was essential for cooking three times a day, year-round. It was a crisis if Mother ran out of wood. She then sent us kids scurrying out into the sagebrush for anything that burned, including big branches of sagebrush that burned so quickly they were of little help.

On those wood-shortage days, Mother must have considered serving Lynn a cold sandwich for the noon meal. But marriages on a ranch didn't operate that way. Mother knew that planting or harvesting a crop — our livelihood — took precedence over all and she would get by somehow until Lynn was able to think about woodpiles.

Nowadays, I miss the sound of wood being chopped as dusk settles in. It bespoke of warmth, security, comfortable routine, and closeness of family.

It shows how far we have come in this labor-saving age. Nowadays, in order to get enough physical activity, it is sometimes necessary to lift weights, swim or walk, and there are few meaningful chores for kids. Nowadays, a thermostat need only be turned.

CHAPTER 23

And You Think 10 Digits Are Bad

Before radio offered soap operas and "The Shadow," and before television offered its vast program potpourri, housewives in rural America derived a fair amount of entertainment from eavesdropping.

Eavesdropping was the stealthy practice of listening to telephone conversations of others on party lines.

A phone in those days was a heavy black rectangle mounted on the wall. We had no phone book. On the wall beside the phone was our handwritten directory: the names of perhaps a dozen or so ranchers on ours, the mountain line. Opposite the names of our neighbors — the nearest was perhaps a mile and a half away — was their number or ring.

We answered our phone when we heard our ring: a short, two longs and a short. To reach Chance and Millie Wilson, we rang three shorts. Every time any one used the phone, we heard the ring. To place a call one took the receiver off the hook and listened to see if anyone was talking, then cranked the handle on the side of the box to effect the ring.

When the ring went out, it was not a personal call. It wasn't a good idea to call a neighbor and badmouth some other neighbor on the line. If Millie Wilson was in the habit of calling Crystal Enright every morning, and Theo Owings wanted to know what was going on in their world, she could ever so gently lift up the receiver, listen in and find out. If one were sufficiently skilled in taking the receiver from the hook, sometimes the talking parties were unaware that another party was on the line.

And, if you were eavesdropper, you wanted to be aware of background noise. If you had the only piano on your line and someone was pounding on the piano, it was a pretty good giveaway. But others, aware that there was no absolute way of detecting the identity of the rubbernecker, brazenly took down the receiver, creating that instantly recognizable sound. Sometimes, eavesdroppers heard uncomplimentary things about themselves: "Well, I guess we have someone else on the line." Or, "Have you noticed that some people just have to know what's going on?" Sometimes the eavesdropper took offense and hung up the receiver with a big bang. More often, there was no response, so the two who were talking were always aware that their conversation was audited.

These conversations, sometimes, were interminable, although the two parties may have talked at length the day before. And, sometimes, these lengthy conversations caused ill feeling among others on the party line. If Slim Owings badly needed more binder twine so he could get on with his binding and needed to phone Monument to see if Boyer's Cash Grocery had any in stock or whether he would have to drive to Long Creek, he might easily lose an hour waiting for the talkers to get off the line.

If they heard, time after time, the loud click of a receiver taken off the hook, and the loud bang when it was replaced, the talkers usually got the message and reluctantly ended their conversation with, "Well, I guess someone wants the line worse than we do." Then, wanting to know who had so rudely interrupted them, they, in turn, sneaked the receiver off the hook to listen and see if the interruption was warranted.

If it was even more of an emergency, one could interrupt the parties on the line and advise that one badly needed to make a call.

Eavesdropping was not usually indulged in by the men. Men mostly were out in the field, riding for cattle or mending fence. And the socializing wasn't because ranch wives had time on their hands. Rather, it was that they might not see another woman for days. Eavesdropping was the same as a coffee break,

One ring that was certain to bring everyone to the phone was our fire ring — the emergency ring — one single long ring. If Stanley Musgrave had a grass fire, his wife Edith could dash to the phone, ring the emergency number and soon expect help.

My mother once got a call from Bill Lesley advising that a rabid coyote was headed toward our ranch. She acted quickly. She herded us kids inside, closed the door and took the .22 rifle down from its rack on the wall, although she could never remember which eye to close when she sighted.

To call someone not on our line, it was necessary to go through Central, a service provided by Boyer's Cash Grocery for a nickel or a dime charge. When Dempsey, or his son Bub, answered, we'd ask him to ring the Neals, the Capons, or the Flowers on the river line, whereupon that number was rung, and the two lines connected.

For a time, long before area codes were known, it was a monumental task for anyone to reach Monument from distant points in the state. If a relative in Portland advised the operator he wanted to call the Lynn Forrests in Monument, usually there was a pause. "Do you mean Monmouth?" the operator often asked. She was assured that Monument was the town. "I don't believe I have a Monument station," she'd say hesitantly. "It's in Grant County. Try going through John Day," we'd advise. But the connecting circuit was not always through John Day. At times, Heppner was the key. And mostly, the connection was so crackly and noisy that long distance calls were made only for urgent reasons.

We could not, of course, carry our phone around with us, or even sit down when we talked. Never at the supper table did one have to answer a call that inquired as to whether we needed siding for our house or had a cracked windshield. There just weren't as many people in those days. And there was no elephant on television to remind us that soon it would be necessary to dial 10 digits to call neighbors across the street.

CHAPTER 24

Good-Bye, Little Red Schoolhouse

Little red schoolhouses don't exist much anymore. Our eastern Oregon schoolhouse was very different from today's grand schools.

Our school building in Monument, that to me then seemed large and was indeed the biggest building in town, had two classrooms for the lower eight grades and two rooms for high school.

Hard-packed dirt surrounded our schoolhouse — no landscaping. Playground equipment included a slide, rings, bars — no track field. We had too few students for football. When we played softball, an X in the dirt was home base. We had no gymnasium and played basketball in the community hall.

For the lower eight grades, the two teachers, traditionally women, each taught four grades. Usually they were Monument residents, often teaching the offspring of students they'd had earlier on.

Kids from Kimberly, Hamilton, Courtrock and Top came to Monument High, a consolidated district — home of the Rimrock Savages. Our principal always was a man; the second teacher, a woman. Our facilities included one large room in which the principal held forth and taught classes. That was our home room and classes went on about us. In the other room, our distaff teacher taught typing, shorthand, English and literature. Adjacent this room was the little typing annex with a window in the door so the teacher could watch us. There, on four manual typewriters, we took speed tests. An auditorium occupied the building's lower level. Commencement, plays and programs were held there.

No lunches were available at school, nor did we have a pop machine.

Town kids went home at noon. The rest packed a lunch or went to Boyer's Cash Grocery for a nickel candy bar. The big boys who rode horseback to school, and wore cowboy boots and hats, didn't hang out around school during lunch. Maybe they went to feed their horses — and perhaps smoke behind the barn.

Our teachers deserved medals of honor. In addition to classes, the female teacher sometimes coached the girls' basketball team, and tried to start a little band consisting of piano, drum and instruments through which we hummed. She rehearsed our plays, and she accompanied us on the piano when we sang at programs.

The teachers had one consolation. Monument had no PTA that required teacher attendance.

Mostly, high-school teachers came from afar. I do not know whether they came for interviews before being hired, but I suspect they were selected from written applications. One hoped they had seen Monument before beginning nine months "incarceration," as some may have regarded it.

Housing was limited. Often, single teachers boarded with a family. Monument was isolated. Roads into town were unpaved until after World War II. We had no bus or train service; no movies or town library; no Lions, Kiwanis, Rotary or Soroptimists.

I'm certain our teachers did not regard it as such, but for us grade school kids, an annual momentous event was the visitation by the county school superintendent. Our teacher stressed how important it was to make a fine showing for Mrs. Boyer.

I was much in awe of young, attractive Mrs. Boyer. I could not keep my place in reading because I kept peering at her: dark, shiny carefully curled hair; navy suit, the epitome of style; shoe heels not even slightly run over. Had I thought it possible, my goal would have been to be a county school superintendent.

Sometimes, coming to Monument was traumatic for new students as well as teachers. When I came as a third grader, the other two third graders, a boy and a girl who grew up in Monument, resented this intrusion. Our desks were not bolted to the floor, but could be slid around the room.

My classmates schemed that if they slid their desks elsewhere and left me behind, they might rid themselves of me. But I badly wanted to be one of them, and wherever they scooted, I scooted, too. In time, that ceased, and the other girl student, Reta Stubblefield, became a best friend. We were the only two in our class through much of grade school, and two of four in our senior graduating class.

People in small towns get to know each other well. Two long-time grade school teachers who taught in adjacent rooms got to know each other too well. One recess, as we students clustered around, the two women became involved in a fight, pulling hair, kicking, shoving and finally knocking each other down.

But the teacher who really wished he'd never seen Monument was our principal, Mr. Hampton. During the school year, he married a woman from out of town. The big "cowboy" students decided it was only neighborly to shivaree the principal, so they tied him with ropes and took him for a horse-back ride; we suspected it was his first.

Isolated though it may have seemed to newcomers, I loved high school.

We did not think of ourselves as underprivileged. Indeed, we were not. Today, if I were a high school student, I would not mind at all going to that little red schoolhouse in Monument.

CHAPTER 25

No Lazy Summer Days on a Ranch

Songwriters rhapsodizing about the lazy days of summer must never have lived on a ranch.

It seemed that my Mother and stepfather, Lynn, spent the entire summer readying for winter.

The biggest summer job was haying, with horses providing the power before the days of tractors and the marvelous machines that neatly pack hay into bales.

Before the "horse power" could be turned on, the animals had to be fed, watered and harnessed. The different steps in haying went on day after day: mowing, raking, shocking — with the biggest job pitching and stacking.

Ranchers who had sons were lucky to have built-in hay hands. Until my little brother became old enough to work in the hay fields, my stepfather had two alternatives. He could hay by himself, driving the team from shock to shock, pitching hay into the wagon and then clambering up in the wagon to occasionally distribute the hay.

Or, lacking money to hire hayhands, he could trade work with a neighboring son-less farmer — in which case the haying went on almost twice as long. If that were the arrangement, Lynn would finish putting up hay on our ranch, and then he would rise before dawn each day and ride horseback to the neighbor's ranch to spend the day haying. Then he'd ride home to do chores at our ranch at night.

Pitching hay on the wagon, it seemed to me, was the nastiest of jobs. Usually it was dusty and blistering hot. The scratchy, itchy hay got down one's neck and up one's long sleeves.

When Lynn and my brother, after he was old enough to help, came in at noon from hauling, we always had two questions: How many loads had they hauled and how many rattlesnakes had they seen? Rattlesnakes often crawled underneath the shocks, perhaps seeking shade or hunting mice, and then were caught up in the hay when it was pitched on the wagon. The person in the wagon never knew when an irate rattlesnake might become part of his load.

Stacking hay also was hard physical work — and competitive. Every rancher examined his neighbor's stack to see if it was neatly and symmetrically formed.

In addition to "lazy days" songwriters sometimes refer to summer as the time for pretzels and beer. That might have been welcomed by eastern Oregon hay hands, but it surely would have surprised them. They were accustomed to water in what had once been a vinegar jug, when they were out in the field

In time, haying became a bit more automated on our ranch with the acquisition of a binder, but it was not self-propelled. This big, lumbering, strange-looking machine had a vile disposition and usually refused to properly tie the bundles of hay. Lynn's haying was constantly interrupted by trips to Long Creek, and even more distant points, seeking parts to repair it.

With haying finally done, Lynn then had to think about gathering and cutting enough wood to feed the heater and cookstove all winter, while playing catch-up with all other jobs left undone: building fence, repairing corrals, riding for cattle.

Meanwhile, back at the ranch, wives cooked three hearty meals a day, with no countenancing of such spur-of-the-moment entrees as creamed tuna on toast. If the apple pie was all eaten at noon, another dessert was stirred up for supper. And before meals could even be started, potatoes had to be dug, peas shelled, carrots pulled and raspberries, for shortcake, picked. Haying was the big job facing men, but "putting up" — canning, preserving, pickling — for the winter was the big job facing wives. They'd used their canned goods all winter and now were faced with a cellar full of empty fruit jars.

Sometimes, if summer didn't run out, ranch families took a vacation of sorts. With team and wagon, families headed for the high mountains to pick huckleberries.

Providing for food and warmth took inestimably more time then, but ranch families must have taken much satisfaction in what they had done. Now they could snuggle down, secure and ready for winter — after fall plowing and seeding was done.

That must have been as satisfying for them as lazing away summer days, even with pretzels and beer.

CHAPTER 26

Dating Was Rough Road

During the Depression, a gal who lived on an eastern Oregon ranch — on a road that was slick as a pig's ear when it rained — had three strikes against her when it came to getting dates.

The dating fellows around Monument, where I lived, knew well the kind of road into every ranch where a datable girl lived.

Said Jim Johnson to Fred Ferringer, "I'd kind of like to ask Nona Jordan to go to the dance Saturday, but the last time I asked her for a date, their road was so bad that her dad had to bring a team of horses down to pull me out. She's a dry-weather date as far as I'm concerned."

Those country roads during the Depression knew no gravel nor grading. There was no money for such. A gal who lived at the end of such a road might have a long dull winter when those roads often were a quagmire that could easily bottom out a car. Even in summer, a driver often had to be careful not to high center a car in the ruts left from winter.

Ranchers mostly drove pickups with lots of clearance, but kids who earned enough money working as hay hands sometimes gave way to a yearning for a cool Chevy or flashy Studebaker, despite their being much less able to navigate the roads into ranches of datable girls.

The condition of the road was not the only factor that had to do with a gal's "datability." She could be pretty as a princess, but if she lived 10 miles or so out of town on a dirt road, distance lessened her chances for dates. George Dietrick, who lived up toward Long Creek, might think twice about asking Emma Thorpe, who lived up in a community called Top, to go to a dance at Spray. Hours of driving, plus using up half a tank of gas, make Emma a poor investment.

True, in those days you could buy gas for maybe 25 cents a gallon. Then, too, just about every ranch had a couple of drums of gasoline for its own supply and a lot of gallons were siphoned from those drums by sons who were dating Emmas, without a father being aware of it.

Not many kids had their own cars. Many rode horses to school although in Monument no guy ever showed up at the house of his date with an extra horse in tow. It wouldn't have been much of a date if Joel Torgerson trotted up to Gladys Trent's home on his sorrel mare and shouted at her from the saddle, "I'm here." Whereupon his date then would have appeared in a pink crepe dress, crawled into the saddle and off they'd ride at a gallop.

Singles— both boys and girls — did sometimes depend on horses to get to a dance. My sister, our girl friends, and I thought it fun to ride horseback to dances at Top — some five miles from our ranch. Those dances were held in a little schoolhouse no longer used for that purpose. Girls did not then wear pantsuits or jeans for any dress-up event, so we carried "good clothes" rolled up on the back of the saddle to change into when we arrived at Top.

We left our horses in a little shed across the county road from the dance hall, where kids generations before had sheltered the horses they rode to school. In that little shed, in the dark, we changed into our dress-up clothes for the dance, peering close at each other, asking if our hair looked all right and if our seams were straight.

After the dance, we changed back into jeans and rode our waiting horses home.

Transportation in Grant County for us kids often posed a problem. My sister was asked to go to a dance up on Top by Earl, a boy who did not have a car. He asked his friend Bill if he would drive Earl and my sister to the dance. Bill was agreeable, and my sister and Earl then obligingly asked me to go along — since I had no date. Bill, the owner of our transportation, asked me at the dance to go to "supper." When I said no, he was upset and wouldn't drive any of us home.

Some high school kids without horse or car — and there weren't many of them — even offered to "walk" a girl home. If a guy walked a girl home, he was more prone to make that suggestion on a balmy summer night rather than in six inches of snow when he had no galoshes. A guy had to know whereof he spoke if he offered to walk a girl home. He couldn't get halfway to her ranch house and then say, "I'm getting a blister on my heel. I'm going back."

Only one boy friend ever walked me home. Our road to the ranch ran rather closely parallel at one point to Monument cemetery and one night as he walked me home, some of his buddies devised the idea of sneaking out to the cemetery ahead of us. As we passed the graveyard, they made weird, spooky sounds and jumped out to scare us to death.

My "walking date" that night was a true gentleman. Other kids, fearful of cemetery ghosts, might have taken off fast as ever they could, leaving their date standing at the cemetery. But not my date. We were quite proud that we gave little satisfaction to those "ghouls."

In addition to distances and conditions of these rural roads, another problem could arise. None of the roads were signed. We had no rural mailboxes with names that might have helped. We picked up our mail at Monument. A guy trying to find his date who lived on a ranch far out of town might drive around a long time before he found the right one.

A friend from Hardman at a dance in Monument one night asked me to go to a dance at Long Creek the following Saturday. He was fun and a good dancer, and I quickly said, "Yes."

For that date, I put up my hair, pressed my dress and was all ready. But on that Saturday night it grew later and later, and no date showed up. Said Mother, "I don't believe your date is coming."

Nor did he. Instead of being "stood up," I preferred to think that he wandered around trying to find the road to our ranch and eventually gave up trying.

That's certainly not to say that there weren't problems with transportation on dates west of the mountains.

On my first date with Homer, who became my husband, we drove to a dance in his Model A, had three flats on the way home and drove in on the rim.

CHAPTER 27

Cruisin' for a Bruisin'

For a time, the Oregon State Police came to about every dance in Monument — and they didn't come to waltz.

Our dances, during the Depression, were one of few social activities other than high school basketball games and school plays. People had scant money to spend on such and cost for the dance they could probably afford: $1 per male, plus cost of "supper" if you wanted to partake of that at midnight. Further, if you were a male who didn't dance, admittance was free—as it was for female attendees. Males had to have somebody to dance with. Even people who didn't dance came to our dances to mingle and socialize. Some came to fight.

These weren't the "buy a ticket, sit around the ring and watch two people demonstrate pugilistic skills" kind of fights. These were the earthy kind where one guy says to another guy whom he doesn't like very well, "I'll see you outside."

Outside, they throw their coats on the ground and go at each other with bare fists as instructions are shouted by "seconds" — friends of those delivering the blows.

Although other Grant County towns must surely have had similar fights at their dances, Monument had the reputation of having the most. That reputation brought State Police to our dances to keep things in hand. Monument had no local police department, no marshal, no members of the National Guard standing by if the situation erupted out of control.

Not all of Monument's fights were fueled by ill feelings between fighters. Many fights were fueled by liquor. Joe Tareyton might come to a dance without a girl and without ever having been on the dance floor in his entire life. That left time for other activities. He came prepared — bringing along a bottle of hooch that he stashed in his car or hid under the edge of the dance hall porch. As the dance began, he socialized. Seeing Jack Abercrombie in the hall — from whom he'd once bought heifers that turned out pretty well -- he invites Jack outside to join him in a little sampling. If these visits outside are frequent, the consumed liquor often stimulates "let's fight" tendencies.

Some of these fights were like serial installments. The same people fought at every dance — the result of a sort of Hatfield and McCoy kind of relationship between families that had disliked each other for so long that they could no longer remember why but felt beholden to carry on the tradition. If at the dance we noticed a bunch of Hatfields saunter in the front door and later the McCoy family members arrived — we knew this was fight night.

Sometimes the fighters' friends — similarly fueled by visits outside — were tempted to jump into the fight, too. The police wanted no free-for-alls erupting into a melee and perhaps resulting in serious injury. They knew there was possibility that these fights might get ugly and that someone might use another weapon if fists weren't getting the job done.

Nor were the Hatfield-McCoy types of fights the only ones. The liquor bottle was a bit like a genie, and from it could come all kinds of reasons for fighting. Young bucks got in fights over girls. If John Stillwater brought Agnes Switherington to the dance — and she'd been going to all the dances hitherto with Paul Prudhome — Paul, if the level of the bottle in his car went down rapidly, might accost John and invite him outside.

Everyone else at the dance knew when these fights erupted. Most male attendees thought a fight was better entertainment than a two-step. When a fight started, the dance hall emptied of males as suddenly as if someone shouted "fire" — leaving inside only elderly wives sitting on the benches and young girls awaiting partners.

We nice girls didn't go outside — except for one eventuality. Our community hall had no rest rooms inside, which necessitated that one go out-side for such. If such a trip became necessary, we asked a girl friend to go along — as a sort of respectability symbol. Nice girls didn't want anyone to think that they were going outside to take a drink or to park with a guy, or to try to peek through the circle of male onlookers to see a little of the fight.

Monument's citizenry was much aware of such trips made outside dur-ing a dance. Everyone in town knew exactly how many times every girl went outside. The morning after a dance when Mother and I discussed the social event, she informed me that Joelene Amsterdam, for example, had left the hall four times and that, indeed, her kidneys must be failing, and that Georgia Rae Folderedge had gone out so many times that Mother had lost track.

Although I never watched those fights, I was somewhat aware of their format. They didn't end up with a referee holding up the arm of the winner. Mostly, we never knew how the fights ended. Perhaps the end was when the fighters got tired and began wondering what this effort was all about. Then Paul might say to John, "You know, I don't mind if you bring Agnes to the dance. Bring her whenever you'd like. I've been wanting to take Trixie out — and I was wondering how to break it off with Agnes."

Monument's unsavory reputation with regard to wild dances didn't hurt attendance — and perhaps increased it. People from Spray, Dayville, Fox, Kimberly, Long Creek, Hardman, Top — sometimes even Lone Rock — came to our dances.

Only a few times did the police arrest anyone. Mostly the combat-ants ended up with bruised knuckles, perhaps a black eye and a torn shirt — although one Hatfield-McCoy participant almost lost an eye in an alter-cation.

These fights as a rule probably weren't as rough as a professional foot-ball game. It was sort of an unwritten code that you didn't kick a downed opponent or jump on him, and it was "unethical" for a fighter's friends or relatives to leap into the fray if their man began to lose the fight.

These fights were about the only way that Monument got its name in the weekly Blue Mountain Eagle — other than that "Fred and Sophie Randall of Monument went to Fox Saturday to buy hay of Fred Jensen." We always read the Monument news first and learned, "Everyone had a great time at the dance in Monument Saturday night. Among those again attending were the State Police who kept an eye on things."

Maybe, those who participated in the fights — such as John and Paul — despite cuts and bruises — went home feeling pretty macho. Then John runs into Eldon Potter at the service station at Long Creek the next week, and Eldon remarks, "I hear you got the better of it with Paul the other night at the dance in Monument."

And John says, with undisguised satisfaction — even though he and Paul had sort of amicably agreed to end the fight— "Yeah, I took care of him pretty good."

CHAPTER 28

Not so Tickled by a Bed of Feathers

I'm glad I've never had to deal with feather beds as part of my housewifely chores. I knew about feather beds while growing up in eastern Oregon. They served as mattresses on all our beds.

I doubt that Mother had seen a feather bed before we moved to Monument, and I suspect she would have quickly discontinued acquaintance if she had had a choice. Our feather beds in Monument must have been handed down several generations on my stepfather's side of the family. Feather beds seemed never to wear out.

Making a feather bed I am sure was a laborious task. One first saved all feathers from chickens and other fowls killed. The choicest small feathers then were separated out and, after a very long time — unless one ate something that was feathered with every meal — sufficient feathers were accumulated to constitute a feather bed.

The bag or sack that held the feathers was of heavy ticking material, usually drab blue-and-white striped, as strong as sail cloth and roughly the size of the bed frame.

Our feather beds had no sections or divisions, and feathers merged together in this one huge sack — not confined to their own little areas as is accomplished with quilting. After one slept on a feather bed, it wilted and lost its buoyancy like a tire that has become flat. Each time the bed was made, it was necessary to throw back all covers and vigorously shake up the feathers, pummeling it this way and that.

If one were to get a passing grade as a housewife, one had to make sure, after the plumping up, that the feather bed, then covered with quilts and bedspread, presented a reasonably smooth top. Otherwise the made-up bed looked like Oregon's topographical map.

If one skipped the daily stirring up of the feathers, they matted down and sleeping on it was like sleeping on an air mattress from which air had escaped.

In addition to the daily shake-up and smoothing, there was the "spring house cleaning" of those heavy feather beds. Somehow they had to be dragged outside and hung over a very strong line or other support, so that all dust could be pummeled from them. As I recall a broom was used for whomping out the dirt. I was never assigned this task, and I suspect that most spring seasons my mother overlooked this portion of her cleaning.

But these disadvantages certainly did not keep me from sleeping soundly and restfully on a feather bed. I have slept on far more uncomfortable beds — especially when we were camping.

Sinking down into a nicely made feather bed is a cozy way to get a good night's rest. I'm just glad I don't have the daily job of whomping up the feathers, getting them smoothed out and undertaking that spring housecleaning.

CHAPTER 29

Springtime Was Tick Time

Over in the Blue Mountains of northeastern Oregon in the spring of the year, the tick had its day.

We didn't know about ticks until we moved to Grant County. But long before we saw one, we heard ominous stories about them. Ticks caused a disease that could be serious, even fatal. We'd never heard of the disease before: Rocky Mountain spotted fever.

Although we saw ticks all year long, it was in the spring that they were as much in evidence as dandelions in an untended lawn.

"Watch out for tick fever," the ranch women told Mother. "It may start with a red rash on the hands and wrists." After the rash came headaches, mental confusion and high fever. And the fever wasn't over in a couple of days. It might last for three weeks.

My Mother wanted to know what a tick looked like and how to safeguard against this Rocky Mountain spotted fever.

"You'll know a tick when you see it," the old-timers said. "It's about as big around as the eraser on a pencil. A little, flat bug, so flat it looks as if it had been pressed between the pages of a book."

We soon discovered that a tick might not stay flat long. Once it attached itself and began helping itself to a person or animal's blood, it puffed up and became as big and bulbous as a plump steamed raisin — and about the same grayish, purplish color.

Mother, already aware that she was living among rattlesnakes and black widow spiders, wondered how one survived among these threats to life. "Well, above all," she was told, "don't just grab hold of a tick and try to pull it out if it has started to bite. If you do that, the body may come off and the head will stay buried under the skin."

Ticks will be most prevalent in the spring, we were told. When the sagebrush bloomed, they seemed at their height, although why they were associated with sagebrush is hard to understand. After all, sagebrush couldn't supply them with blood.

It wasn't long before we were introduced to ticks firsthand. I went for a hike in the sagebrush, took off my jacket when I got home and there, crawling on my arm slowly, determinedly, was a little flat bug. I knew what it was at once. This air-breathing animal that's related to spiders has all its body parts in one piece. It can't fly and doesn't move fast enough to alarm, but you can't brush it off as you might a spider. They cling and stick.

I called Mother and told her I thought a tick was on my arm. She rushed to save me, and called my stepfather, Lynn, who knew all about ticks from living many years in eastern Oregon. Lynn picked the tick off my arm, took it to the woodstove, dropped it on the hottest part and it sizzled to death. "You can't do that if it's bitten you," Lynn said. He suggested that Mother and I check my clothing and body to see if any more were crawling round. I found two: one on the sleeve of my jacket and one on my pant leg. Tick season was under way.

My sister was the first to discover that she had been bitten by a tick. She felt something on the back of her shoulder that she couldn't see — something bulbous — and told Mother. She was horrified. This creature imbedded in my sister's shoulder, could no longer be identified as a tick. All body markings and characteristics were gone, and it now looked like an over-blown balloon that could burst at any time.

Mother knew she shouldn't try to quickly pull it off. She grabbed a wooden match, lighted it and let it burn until it was hot, then blew out the flame, told my sister to hold still and applied the hot end of the match to the tick. It quickly gave up its food supply as it felt that red hot poker and immediately backed out. Mother, hating to pick up that awful-looking thing, grabbed it and ran quickly to drop it on the stove.

Now we knew about ticks. We just hoped my sister wouldn't come down with Rocky Mountain spotted fever. When Mother started checking around, she was relieved that few locals had caught the disease, but that didn't lessen our watchfulness for the carrier. After we'd been outside, especially after walking through the sagebrush or being around the horses, sheep or other animals, we checked our clothing and bodies. Sometimes, at the height of the season, we'd find six or eight of the little creatures trying to find a food supply.

After a season or so, we learned to live with the ticks without much fear of them, just as we got along with black widows and rattlesnakes in the summer.

But just as I always worried that an earwig would get in my ear, so, too, I worried as to what would happen if I inadvertently knocked the body off a tick and its head stayed imbedded in me. I was concerned about how much of my surrounding body would need to be removed to get rid of that burrowed-in head. I was comforted when no old-timers could tell me of such a happening.

Since those days in eastern Oregon, a tick research laboratory was established at Rhode Island University. It noted that, next to mosquitoes, ticks transmit the greatest variety of disease-producing organisms causing Rocky Mountain spotted fever rickettsiae, babesiosis piroplasms, and Lyme disease spirochetes in the Northeast. Lyme disease was rated as the most prevalent arthropod-borne disease in North America and a significant threat in public health.

To me, rats seem a more odious carrier than ticks, so I was almost glad to read that ticks have crowded out rats as a spreader of disease. And I've never seen a tick in Oregon's Willamette Valley.

But if you do find a tick with head imbedded in your body, I'm now advised that a drop of alcohol or turpentine applied to the offensive critter is said to work as well as that eastern Oregon hot match.

CHAPTER 30

The John Day: Free Entertainment

We kids in eastern Oregon wanted summer never to end. Our swim pool, the John Day River, became ugly at summer's end, and our mothers would no longer let us swim in it for fear it was polluted. Without a real swim pool, during summer the river offered our finest entertainment.

The John Day at Monument provided a fine swimming hole. The bank sloped down gradually with a sandy bottom so that we didn't stab our toes on rocks as we minced into the water.

An old lean-to shed provided some privacy for us girls changing into swim suits. The boys' dressing room was a large room-like opening in a cliff about 10 feet above the water, and around the bend from our shed.

From upstream in the river, the boy's dressing room was visible, so if boys came to swim, we stayed downstream until we heard them dive in. We would have been embarrassed to view their dressing room when it was occupied. If girls unknowingly swam upstream when a boy had been slow getting into his swim trunks, the guffaws of his companions were heard all over the river.

Almost every summer day after our noon meal, I walked the mile and a half to the swimming hole. Our facility required no pre-rinse showers. Sometimes I wore a swimsuit to town under my clothes. One advantage of wearing home a wet suit was that for a little while it kept one cool.

The girls' dressing room, although it offered some privacy, had disadvantages. The shed often housed farm animals which made it prudent to leave on shoes until one reached the river's edge.

The boys' facility, in addition to being less than private, had another disadvantage. From their rocky dressing room, they had to dive the 10 feet or so into the river, mandating the wet-all-at-once approach.

In this respect we girls had the advantage of being able to hesitatingly enter the river step by step, holding our breath as the water reached our waist and splashing water on arms to reduce shock of forthcoming immersion. Or, we, too, could choose to bravely leap in.

Although we had no lifeguard, no one drowned during those years when we swam in the river almost every summer day. Nor had any of us had Red Cross life-saving classes. Had classes been available, we wouldn't have thought we needed them. We were good swimmers and when I headed for the river, I never heard the motherly admonition, "Now don't go in over your head."

During the winter, the John Day became ugly. Sometimes it flooded lowlands. It took out the bridge at Monument several times. During prolonged cold periods, it froze so hard that teams of horses could use it as a thoroughfare.

But toward the end of spring, as the water cleared and was warmed by the sun, we kids began to anxiously await the opening of our pool.

Early in the season, the John Day was not a friendly host. Melting snow in the Blue Mountains limited our swim to popping in the river, barely getting wet and clambering out, blue with cold and trying to catch our breath.

But as summer came and the sun hovered at the 100-degree mark, the river warmed, bid us welcome, and by mid-summer, after walking to town, the river's cool was a joy.

Our daily swim lasted until late in the afternoon. We'd see how many times we could swim across the river until, teeth chattering, we headed for the sand, baking alternately front and back, believing in those days that the sun's rays were beneficial.

Sometimes we dozed in the sun, but more often we discussed all manner of things, including what we were going to be when we grew up.

Late in the summer, the John Day turned surly again as if it were tired of being used. Its clear fast-running water grew lazy and became putrid green. Leaves and debris lazily accumulated in places where the water never moved. The river level dropped, so that some years we could touch bottom all the way across.

We dreaded our mothers' announcement that we could no longer use the river because they feared it was polluted. We never had the benefit of health department tests to determine whether our mothers were right. But secretly we acknowledged it was less pleasant to swim in that river when it was pea green.

Fall brought the start of school so we didn't long sorrow over closure of our swimming facility.

But as winter moved in, we remembered swimming in the bright clear waters of the John Day and baking in the sun. During the Depression that was a godsend when money was short and entertainment scarce. That was entertainment that every kid should experience.

CHAPTER 31

Lessons of Valentine's Day

Our grade school teachers at Monument may not have realized that our Valentine's Day box taught us kids valuable lessons about life.

A couple of weeks before February 14, the big red and white cardboard container with the large slot in the top was positioned prominently at the front of the room.

Valentine's Day was different from other important days at school because no lesson concerning it was doled out. On Thanksgiving Day, we heard again about the pilgrims, although we knew that story pretty well. On November 11, we heard about World War I. On Lincoln's and Washington's birthdays, we studied their accomplishments. But not many of us knew why we had a Valentine's Day box.

We later realized that on that day, we learned lessons, such as how to decide which kids would get our nicest valentines and whether kids who hadn't been very nice to us deserved any valentine at all.

But uppermost in our minds was the question of how many valentines we, ourselves, would get.

The valentines we deposited in the box weren't bought at a Hallmark store. In Monument, it was necessary to catalog-order a valentine-card kit, from which we crafted the cards that we gave. Every night for a week or two before that important day, we cut and glued and put together lovely cards for our classmates, all the time thinking about whom we would give them to. If we botched one, it might be OK for Gilbert, who laughed at the answer I gave in history class.

After I "allocated" my nicest cards — perhaps a half-dozen fancy ones — the quality of those remaining deteriorated considerably in size, prettiness and elegance.

A few days before February 14, we brought our cards to school. When we saw Jolene importantly put a handful of valentines in the box, we'd wonder if she were putting in one for us. She knew that I'd asked Lulu to stay all night twice, and I'd asked her only once this year.

When I had troubles deciding about valentine dispensation, I consulted Mother.

"Gertrude is really my best friend," I said, "but she ate lunch twice with Priscilla last week and I don't think a best friend would do that. Maybe I shouldn't give her my nicest valentine but my third favorite one."

Mother wondered if perhaps Gertrude felt hurt because I'd asked Gloria to work on a class project instead of Gertrude and that maybe it would be a good idea to give her a really nice card to show I didn't mean anything by that.

I gave Gertrude my second nicest card, and then I consulted Mother again to see whether to give Hattie a card.

"She hasn't lived here very long, and she hardly even says hello to me." I said.

Mother thought maybe if I'd make it a point to talk to Hattie, Hattie would talk to me and think of me as a friend. So I gave Hattie one of my not so nice cards.

The opening of the Valentine's Day box came after classes on February 14, or if it was on a weekend, we observed a big Friday. After the teacher designated two or three kids to distribute cards, one of the important events of the school year started. In large measure, it might determine social strata. If I got fewer valentines than Patty, everyone would know. We had a good idea of how many stops the kids distributing valentines made at everyone's desk. If they made more stops at Gertrude's desk than mine, I began to shrink down in my desk with a miserable attack of the "no one likes me" syndrome.

As Priscilla oohed and aahed about the beautiful valentine that Gertrude had given her, I was pretty sure that the one Gertrude had given me wasn't nearly as pretty, so maybe she wasn't my best friend, after all. And Patrick, whom I had thought perhaps fancied me, wrote no message on the valentine he gave me. He signed only his name.

We secretly counted our cards as they were delivered to our desks, and it was a successful Valentine's Day when you had a card from everyone in the room.

If I got only 21 cards, and there were 25 kids in our school, it was not a good year. Then, dejectedly, I carried home my sorry collection and hoped I would not cry when I told Mother that things had not gone well.

"Did you give a card to everyone?" Mother asked.

I remembered that I'd ruined a couple of cards when I tried to glue the doily-like material on them and consequently ran out and couldn't give a card to Alex or Juanita.

"Maybe the kids who didn't give you a card ran out, too," Mother said.

"That means I was their worst friend in the whole room," I said. Mother gave me a hug and said she was sorry I got only 21 and not to feel too bad about it. She suggested that if I wanted a nicer card from Gertrude next year, maybe I should ask her to work on a project instead of asking Gloria. She wondered if I'd written anything on Patrick's card, and I hadn't because I couldn't think of anything to write. And it was Mother's idea that if I wanted to get a card from everyone, maybe I should send one to everyone in school.

And so, that disappointing Valentine's Day came to a close. The next year I asked Gertrude, my best friend, to work on a project and I got a really beautiful valentine from her. And Patrick wrote on his card, "Be My Valentine," and I got a card from everyone in school.

But Mother had been right about that disappointing Valentine's Day. A couple of months later, it didn't seem like a terrible tragedy, and in time, I realized that that Valentine's Day had taught me a few things.

The fact that I got only 21 valentines that year, that Gertrude hadn't given me her most beautiful card, that Patrick signed only his name on his valentine, in reality did not change the world. I learned, too, that it was a lot nicer the following year when all those good things came to pass.

CHAPTER 32

Bonding Over Dirty Dishes

Please don't take my dishwasher from me despite this admission: There are benefits of washing and drying by hand.

Long before the era of dishwashers, my sister and I did the dishwashing at our eastern Oregon ranch. We took turns. One meal, I washed and she dried. At the next meal, we switched.

Both of us much preferred the drying job. The washer of the dishes had to do all the pans, as well as to remember to fill the dishpan with water and put it on the woodstove before we sat down to eat. We had no wire drying racks and the shallow pan in which we rinsed the dishes — used also for baking sourdough biscuits — offered a challenge if one were to meticulously immerse the entire dish in rinse water.

An adage contends that a good dish-dryer takes care of any food left on dishes by the dishwasher, but my sister and I did not observe that practice. We delighted in sending back to the dishwasher any silverware, dish or pan with even a tiny bit of food thereon.

This occasionally led to bitter sisterly disagreements. The number of dishes sent back to the dishwasher was moderated only by the realization that we would be dishwasher at the next meal.

It was good that my Mother stayed out of the kitchen during the dishwashing procedure. She did not then have to settle sisterly disputes about whether a dish was clean. Nor did she see the mode of operation. If there were a good many dishes and we had something fried or greasy at our meal

— which was often the case — the dishwater by the time the pans were washed was greasy and gray.

And the quantity of dishes my sister and I could dry with one dishtowel was astonishing. Ours were not dainty tea towels. Our dishtowels were flour sacks graced with the name "Kitchen Queen" and the picture of a smiling housewife. Those markings stayed on through repeated washings. Kitchen Queen's smile began to fade only about the time the dishtowel had worn so thin it was relegated to window washing.

When the dishwashing job was done, the dripping dishtowel hung on a little rack in the corner behind the stove where, despite its saturated state, it was always dry before the next meal.

One problem, never resolved, with regard to whose turn it was to wash, was if my sister or I were gone. If Lillian spent the night with Leola, upon her return I contended that it was her turn to wash. Lillian argued that she had washed the dishes Wednesday noon before she went to stay with Leola, and hence when she came back, it was my turn. Mother occasionally had to mediate these disagreements.

But mostly there was a camaraderie about this washing-drying task. Mostly, we discussed friends, or boyfriends if we had any at the moment, and what clothes we would order from the catalog if given the opportunity, and all sorts of confidentialities.

And there was a satisfaction about that job. You could easily see your accomplishments: a shambles of a kitchen now clean; dishes — only a little bit damp — stacked in the cupboard; the oilcloth-covered table wiped clean. The writer Christopher Morley must also have known that there was camaraderie in the dishwashing job. He wrote, "The man who has never in his life washed the dishes with his wife or polished up the silver plate — he still is largely celibate."

In married life, at our lake cabin, we had no electric dishwasher. But after a picnic or company dinner, the washing and drying was almost fun. One forgot it was a chore because of the companionship. If we had big groups, the washer of the dishes hustled to keep up with the three or four dryers who stood at the ready. Washing and drying did not interfere with exchange of intimate revelations, secrets, recipes and house-decorating ideas.

When our son, Mitch, was growing up, he was the dish wiper and I washed. Jobs for boys were fewer than if we had lived on a ranch. He might not have agreed but those sessions to me were enjoyable.

One year when we planned a vacation in Mexico, we bought a Berlitz self-teaching Spanish book. As we did the dishes, with the book open on the counter, we practiced our Spanish: Hello. How are you? Where is the rest room? How much does it cost?

We could scarcely wait to test our Spanish during that vacation. At a Mexican market, I tried out my skills. I saw a piece of pottery I liked and, in my best Spanish, asked how much it cost. The shopkeeper advised the price in excellent English. Mitch, standing nearby, thought that hilarious.

Don't get me wrong. I surely don't want to give up my dishwasher. It's just that looking back, dishwashing and drying by hand had benefits — even though they were not always appreciated at that time.

CHAPTER 33

Looking Beyond the Lawn

Mother gave up indoor bathroom, electric lights, sidewalks and green lawns when she married my stepfather, Lynn, and moved to eastern Oregon during the Depression.

Our new home was a vast and virginal section of land, mostly sagebrush and juniper, never before farmed. Its 640 acres had no roads and no place for us to live until our two-room house went up one weekend when neighborly ranchers came for a house raising.

From our new home, we looked across a sweeping expanse toward Monument, a mile and a half away. As the sun crept up each morning over Monument Mountain to the east, ours was the first ranch it found. South toward Hamilton and Long Creek, the Blue Mountains formed a panoramic timbered backdrop.

Now, with a roof over our heads, Lynn could think about converting our sagebrush-covered land into a paying ranch. It was good land, carpeted with bunch grass and needle grass. Once cleared it would provide hundreds of acres for rye and wheat.

But sagebrush had to be grubbed out before crops could be planted. Corrals, fences, a chicken house, shed and watering troughs first had to be built before we could have livestock. Although Mother and Lynn started with ready-made family, they had little else: no farm machinery, no livestock, not enough resources to hire work done. And over all hovered the Depression.

Lynn, previously a bachelor, worried about what to undertake first to assure a cash crop, but Mother worried about other things. She could do nothing about piping water to the house from the spring up on the hill, or replacing kerosene lamps with electricity. Nor could she put up a fence around our yard or plow and seed a lawn. But for Mother a home was not complete without lawn.

But she could plant something else green: flowers, shrubs, trees around our stark little house to offset that baked-ground yard. When she wasn't shelling peas, washing, ironing, baking, canning, she spaded flower beds.

The loamy and fertile land, which had known only range grass and sagebrush, was as ready as Mother to provide beautification. When neighbors offered iris bulbs, starts of a climbing yellow rose, lilac, snowballs and matrimonial vine to plant at our outhouse, Mother's own Butchart Garden was under way. Flowers and bulbs were duly planted and each day she carried buckets of water to water them by hand.

After supper, when dishes were done, Mother often took the family on tours of her flower gardens pointing out each new sprout and growth. And always she added, "Won't this look nice when we get a lawn?"

But as the sagebrush was cleared and our 640 acres became a ranch with cattle, horses, dogs, cats, chickens and sheep, Mother, new to this ranching game, came to more fully recognize the difficulties ahead. As the lilac sent forth shoots, a ewe wandered into the unfenced yard and nipped the tender green.

The roses that she planted where the yard fence someday was to be, bravely sent out new growth and Mother smiled and said, "Isn't that about the nicest Mother's Day present that anyone could have?" Then, a frisky calf took off through her rose garden, breaking off most at the ground.

She planted flower seeds and along came hens and their chicks and scratched them out. She replanted and put stakes around the beds, and the chickens came back two days after she replanted.

She tried to train our cattle dogs to chase away the hens when they came into our yard. If someone was watching, the dogs occasionally roused themselves to do so for their "good dog" reward. But when hot weather came, they dug cooling wallows where Mother planted iris bulbs.

When finances permitted, Mother bought shade trees to set out near the house, watering them by hand. As surely as a tree began to flourish, cattle or horses ate the growth or broke it off. And all this while she waited for a lawn to materialize.

But despite setbacks, Mother had wins. A giant lilac bloomed at the back of the house where we could sling out a wash basin of water on it when the window was open. Her flower garden between the cellar and the vegetable garden was an oasis of color and on summer evenings, she insisted that the family come see her flowers, not yet surrounded by lawn.

There came a time when Lynn, having cleared hundreds of acres, having plowed that ground and now concerned only with planting, harvesting, caring for livestock and endless other ranch tasks, squandered time to build a fence around our yard. Mother still wasn't totally victorious. One of us kids would leave the gate open and a calf would sneak in. The dogs still dug cooling holes in her prized flower beds. Cats slept among her choice plants. And still, except for flowers, shrubs and trees, she looked out at a packed-dirt brown yard.

Here at this ranch in Monument Basin, Mother and Lynn lived some 30 years before moving to their other ranch on the North Fork of the John Day. Much change marked those 30 years. My sister and I left to go to school. My brother went to Vietnam. And Mother also underwent change. After 30 years, she began to no longer visualize a green lawn — not because of flagging spirit but because she began looking past the bare-earth yard.

She looked beyond to the wheat fields and on toward the indigo-haze of the Blues and their dark fringe of timber. She looked to the east, at the beauty of the rugged rimrocks that changed hourly as the light played on them. And she began to recognize that this was the most beautiful yard that anyone could have, a lawn that no one could plant.

Although one should not easily give up one's dreams, and although Mother never had her lawn, there is something to be said about looking out and beyond. Look beyond and consider: We may long yearn for lush green lawns but perhaps if we but look more closely, something infinitely better is at hand.

CHAPTER 34

My Horse Was No Sports Car

I never had a red convertible when I was in high school but I had a horse.

Few of my high school friends did have cars. If kids in Monument had vehicles to drive, most often they belonged to their parents. But every kid had a horse to ride — whether or not it was his own.

At that time, Monument ranchers weren't much into genetics. No one had purebred horses. Mostly they had cow ponies — no ongoing breeding programs, no artificial insemination. Nature mostly just took its course.

But despite few equine blue bloods, an eastern Oregon rancher was judged by his saddle horse. A rider wanted a saddle horse of which he could be proud. It was nice, of course, to have a good-looking horse, but to many horse owners, the first requirement was speed.

The rancher who early on was most interested in fine horses in our part of Oregon lived long before we moved there. J. H. Hamilton, in 1874 settled about 10 miles from Monument, midway to Long Creek. That pioneer stockman was the first settler in the area and the community then took Hamilton as its name. According to Grant County lore, it was the custom for everyone in the area to take a favorite horse to his ranch for races — to see if they could best the Hamilton string.

Only occasionally at Monument did we have horse races — and then they were of a pick-up kind. At a Fourth of July get-together, Bill Freeborn might lean back on his haunches, roll a cigarette and say to Dude McDaniel, "You know, Dude, that little bay mare I've got is about the fastest thing on four legs." Whereupon Dude McDaniel would aver that he was pretty sure that bay couldn't keep up with his 2-year-old sorrel gelding. And then Milt Gibson from the ranch up the river would take offense and say that neither of those horses could keep up with his 3-year-old roan.

"Well, why don't we see about that," Bill would say — so they'd agree that Sunday next they'd find out at Monument.

There was no race track at Monument, so they raced in a big summer-fallow field adjacent the school.

During the week, word got around and everyone came Sunday to see whose horse was fastest. Everyone had an opinion about whose horse would win. Several others, who also thought their horse was the fastest, always showed up, including Jim Douglas who was positive his skewbald would come in first. On Sunday, quite a crowd arrived because there weren't many other places to go in Monument or many good excuses to get away from ranch work. But even those who couldn't come to the race heard about the winner and that horse became renowned in the neighborhood.

Chance Wilson, who lived on Top, had a bay admired by everyone. That singlefoot moved along as smooth as a set bowl of Jell-O. There was no up and down motion when Chance and that horse glided along.

It was nice to have a saddle horse that stepped out proudly, held its head high, pranced as if it were in a parade and even sashayed a bit if the wind suddenly blew a piece of paper or a tumbleweed in its path.

Actually, the horse I rode, not solely my own, had few of those attributes. My stepfather, Lynn, had his saddle horse that no one else rode, and our other two saddle horses, Bubbles and Skinner, were shared by my mother, sister, me and my younger brother when he was old enough to ride. When Bubbles filled in as a work horse, I rode Skinner — and Skinner was no red convertible. He wasn't bad looking and he was patient and dependable, but he was a plodder. Only when he was switched did he move out of a walk.

Ordinarily, Skinner's head drooped to a level about even with his knees, so that when I rode him to town and suspected someone might be watching, I pulled tight on the reins to hold his head up like a parade horse. It took utmost persuasion to get him into a gallop, which was of such short duration and of so much effort, it seldom was his gait. We did not think he was of an advanced age. We suspected he was lazy.

Often, some eight or 10 of us high school kids got together on a weekend or on a summer night to ride — perhaps down to the dam to swim. In the eastern Oregon night we'd gallop pell-mell down the trail — and inevitably old Skinner and I would ingloriously bring up the rear as I tried my best to evoke from him a gallop.

I didn't dream of a convertible — but of a spirited animal — preferably a palomino — whose pale mane and tail streamed out behind as we headed the group galloping down the trail.

It was not really necessary that I have a fine horse. I needed him only for transportation, and Skinner provided that — albeit slowly.

Some high school boys had saddle horses that were indeed more than transportation. They were working cattle horses, alert, intelligent, quick.

Skinner was not a red convertible type of horse but I thought a lot of him. I never had a sports car in high school but Skinner, you might say, was my beloved, beat-up old Model T.

CHAPTER 35

A Match Made in Heaven

Some may think that in eastern Oregon we lived in a world of cowboys, cattle and sagebrush. Rather it was a world of wooden matches. On the kitchen wall of our ranch house, a little metal container held a box of Diamond wooden matches. That container represented the heart and soul of our ranch life.

You don't see many wooden matches anymore. Nowadays, if we want a match, which isn't often, we look to the paper variety — enough to make a fine Diamond wooden match cringe in distaste.

Advertising brought that about. We don't buy our paper matches. They're imprinted with the names of motels, restaurants, bars, hotels. Some people make a bobby of collecting the paper variety. They have huge jars filled with match packets from all over the world.

We didn't have paper matches in eastern Oregon. Instead, on the night stand beside every bed was a little pile or saucer of wooden matches. When it was time to get up in the morning, you could in the dark reach out and readily find a match to light the coal oil lamp. Our day started with the lighting of that wooden match.

Matches then lit the fires in heating stove and cookstove.

Of a morning, I'd lie in bed burrowed into a feather-bed mattress, weighted down with comforters, and listen to Lynn, my stepfather, lay the fire. I could then distinctly hear the wooden match as he struck it across the top of the stove. Usually, it took only one of those good wooden matches to start the fire.

Matches got our day off to a fine start — and they continued to be used throughout the day. Those wooden matches were lifesavers.

On a bitterly cold day, when a rancher rode for cattle up on the flats of Johnny Cake and his feet were chunks of ice and his hands so numb he could scarcely hold the reins, wooden matches "rescued" him. He needed only to find a rabbitbrush, crawl stiffly from his horse, dig a match from his pocket and set fire to one of those dried bushes. Even in damp weather, they flared into immediate intense warmth. A lifesaver.

Homer learned about the worth of a wooden match when he hunted on horseback with Lynn. On long hunts, when Homer yearned for down-filled saddles and his legs felt as if they no longer belonged to his body, if they rode by a spring in the breaks of Slickear Mountain, Lynn might call out over his shoulder as to whether Homer was ready for a cup of coffee.

Homer saw no Starbucks at hand, but coffee sounded like a godsend, so they crawled from their horses. From a flour sack on his saddle, Lynn took an empty coffee can. He filled it with water from the spring, dumped in a goodly amount of coffee from a little sack on the saddle, threw together some dried sagebrush and mahogany — and with the light from a single wooden match, they soon had boiling, potent coffee.

Wooden matches were handy, too, especially in the spring during tick season. When we discovered on our person a tick with head embedded and body looking like a plump purplish raisin, we lit a wooden match, waited for it to become a glowing torch, and held it against the body of the tick. It quickly backed out of its position — head and all — and that offending creature was burned at the stake.

Ranchers and cowboys also depended on wooden matches as tooth-picks — the unsulphured end in the mouth. Wooden matches made sturdy toothpicks and provided lots of chewing for thought. If something smaller and more refined was needed to reach into the remoter areas of the mouth, out came the pocket knife and the wooden match was whittled exactly to need. No molar or bicuspid could go unreached with a custom-made Diamond toothpick.

Always in every rancher's pocket was a supply of wooden matches. Most ranchers smoked and, mostly, they rolled their own. Out of the shirt pocket came a little packet of cigarette papers from which they took one. Then from a Bull Durham sack, they sprinkled tobacco down the center of the paper, licked one edge, rolled it up neatly — and lit it with a wooden match.

The way they lit that match was an indicator of how long they'd lived in eastern Oregon. Old-timers could bring a match across the thigh of their jeans, with a firm sweeping gesture, and the match would ignite. The leg of their jeans was a bit worn and showed a powdery residue of sulphur— a sort of macho mark of distinction.

Some also lighted wooden matches under the edge of a fingernail. If a novice tried that, he usually ended up with charred fingertip.

Nowadays, if one smokes cigarettes, they are usually lit with a lighter. No longer do you strike a match every time you turn on the gas stove. Barbecue starters replace matches as starters for that task. Wood fires in fireplaces are giving way to fireplace logs that flare up without matches. Even for jobs still requiring a match, paper matches are replacing the wooden variety — and that's hard to understand.

Paper matches often are hard to light. The flimsy roughened surface at the bottom of the pack often requires two or three swipes to light a match. The paper matches are short. They usually have to be blown out before you get the intended job done — or fingers will be burned. When lighting candles for dinner, it may take several tries to light a single candle with a paper match. If you're having a birthday party for an 80-year-old, you may burn up the matchbook trying to light the candles with paper matches.

There's a legend about the many uses of a cowboy's hat — said to be the most useful object he owned. It kept his head warm and shielded him from the sun and the rain. He could whack his horse on the rump with it to encourage it to move faster. He could use his cowboy hat to get a drink from a watering hole, lacking a cup.

But useful though cowboy hats were, they could not match the uses of a good wooden match.

In our house today, there is no box of wooden matches.

It is difficult to believe that the Diamond match, once so necessary to our eastern Oregon way of life, seems now to be coming to an inglorious end.

CHAPTER 36

End of Winter Brings, Ugh, the Greens

Spring is a joyous season, possibly the best. But one part of spring that I hated as a child was mustard greens.

During a hard winter at our ranch in eastern Oregon, the snow might lay on the ground for weeks. And with its melting it was a delight to again see the ground.

Now with the snow gone my stepfather anxiously assessed the sprouting grass and its growth. Growth of that grass determined when he could stop feeding hay to the cattle. Not only was that a chore nice to have finished, but hay represented cash.

With the melting of the snow, he also could check progress of our winter wheat. Hopefully it had not frozen and would be nicely above ground, indicative of a crop that would mean we wouldn't have to buy hay. With winter's end, too, we could look forward to variation in our diet.

Mostly we were self-sufficient with regard to food — fruits and vegetables were scant on our table, as was the assortment at Monument's one grocery store.

Our mundane diet included potatoes, onions, winter squash, winter cabbage — all stored in the cellar. Dried beans and dried prunes were always a possibility, backed up by tomatoes, and fruits Mother canned: applesauce, pears, peaches, Italian prunes. But other than tomatoes, Mother canned no vegetables. She must have once known a green-bean canner who gave her family ptomaine poisoning. She was the only ranch wife around who did not have rows of quart jars of string beans in her cellar. Mother didn't want to chance giving food poisoning to her family with open-kettle canned vegetables.

Although in those days the importance of a diet that included daily five fruits and vegetables did not receive the play of later years, my Mother nonetheless worried about greens in our fare. She wanted no member of her family to have tired blood. Supplemental vitamins we'd scarcely heard of — although my younger sister and brother received daily dispensation of cod-liver oil.

Some mothers dosed out sulphur and molasses as a spring tonic. I was glad Mother did not do that.

As the snow melted in the spring, Mother also looked expectantly at the ground — not to check the growth of grass for the cattle, but to look for mustard and dandelion greens to put on our table.

Those plants grew in abundance on our ranch every spring, especially around our house where sagebrush and mahogany had been slashed away. Those plants hugged the ground as if they did not want to be dug up, but Mother was a determined provider. With paring knife and grey enamel-ware pan, and me as her unwilling helper, she set out to harvest her greens crop.

I was unwilling — but not because I minded helping with the task. Actually it was enjoyable to be outside after having been captive much of the winter.

The repugnant part of this harvesting, was that Mother at the next meal, expected us to eat them. I liked most things that Mother sat before me except rice pudding and oatmeal, but mustard greens especially, I detested. I abhorred their prickly surface, suggestive of eating the fuzz on a peach. If one managed to forget their prickliness, the slightly pungent flavor was equally abhorrent.

One good thing about those mustard greens was that they cooked down considerably. Although Mother might come back to the house with a large pan of them, by the time they were washed and cooked, they wilted down to a much diminished amount.

Mother was careful to see that each of her family received a portion of the distasteful fare — although always I hoped my stepfather would want to eat all of them. He put a little vinegar on his mustard greens and seemed to relish them.

I, who detested each bite, would greatly have preferred the tired blood that Mother talked about. Whatever size of serving she put on my plate was too large. She heard not my remonstrances although surely she could see that those mustard greens scarcely obeyed my command to stay down.

My salvation was that the harvest of mustard and dandelion greens was brief. After their first rapid growth in the spring, we had only a few servings — far too many for me.

I was grateful to Mother for trying to thwart "tired blood" in her family although I did not believe that my blood was fatigued, or that anything as distasteful as mustard greens could have helped.

The mustard green harvest served one purpose as far as I was concerned: I was so glad to have that over that I didn't much notice the end of that wonderful season — Spring.

CHAPTER 37

When Tuesdays Were for Ironing

Most of my high school girl friends in Monument had a hope chest — preparatory to the wedding which they hoped would be forthcoming some day. In almost every hope chest were sets of tea towels — one for every day of the week. Embroidered thereon was the day of the week, and the related task — to preclude the homemaker's doing the wrong task on any given day. Monday was wash day. Tuesday was for ironing, etc.

A housewife had an ironclad schedule. If she didn't do the wash on Monday and iron on Tuesday, it was almost grounds for divorce. And in those days before no-iron materials and wash-and-wear, if the ironing was to be done efficiently, the clothes had to be sprinkled on Monday night.

Some homemakers had bottles with holes in the lid so one could daintily sprinkle water on the unironed garments as one sprinkles salt on a fried egg. In our home, we used a bowl of water, dipped our fingers in it and splashed the drops on the clothes like an orchestra conductor. This was no menial task that could be entrusted just to anyone.

The success of Tuesday ironing largely depended on how expertly the sprinkling was done. If you dabbled on too much water and the unironed garments were too wet, it took forever to iron the garment dry. If the clothes were too dry, in those days before steam irons, it was almost impossible to coax out the wrinkles.

My grandmother had a huge wicker basket in which the sprinkled clothes were tucked in for the night. A folded bedsheet lined the basket as insulation to keep the sprinkled clothes from drying out. As each item was sprinkled, it was rolled up like a burrito and snugged down in the basket. In big families, that basket would almost be filled. Another folded sheet covered all and the moisture then would become evenly distributed.

Tuesday morning, even if the world were scheduled to end, the ironing got under way. No blue-ribbon wife contemplated playing bridge or golf or going to the mall. Nor would any dutiful wife have issued to a friend such a Tuesday invitation.

In those days before electric irons, much attention had to be given to heating the irons. We used sadirons heated on our wood-burning cookstove. Some of the mothers of my school friends had complex-looking irons that burned fuel, but my Mother did not trust such mechanisms, so we had sadirons. Always I wondered how sadirons came by that name. I decided most homemakers must so dislike ironing that it was regarded as a sad occasion, a sad day

Sadirons — little known now — were pointed at both ends like the hull of a boat and had little removable handles that picked the iron off the stove and released it, back on the stove, after it had cooled.

In order to have an iron of proper temperature, the fire had to be carefully orchestrated. One couldn't iron if the fire went out. And if heated over a roaring fire, a sadiron, which of course had no thermostat, could become too hot. An experienced homemaker first tested the iron on the far end of the ironing board cover where the sadiron rested in its little metal stand.

When I was old enough for Mother to assign to me some of the Tuesday ironing task, I didn't spend all that time ironing. I spent more time searching in the basket for desired pieces to iron — or rather to avoid those I chose not to iron. Pillow cases were my favorites. And the flour sack dishtowels were not difficult to iron. Tablecloths, if not huge, were acceptable and aprons I could deal with.

But when only white shirts, housedresses and blouses with puffed sleeves remained, I gladly would have skipped Tuesdays and gone right to Wednesday.

Surely the designer who fashioned puffed sleeves never had to iron them.

Last week, I found stored away in a drawer some embroidered tea towels that had belonged to Homer's grandmother and on one was a "Monday wash day" design.

I showed them to Homer. "These are wonderful keepsakes," I said. "But why do you think they designated these specific days for those jobs? I don't wash any more often on Monday than any other day, and I certainly don't necessarily iron on Tuesday."

"Maybe it wasn't the homemaker who dreamed up that routine. Maybe it was the husband," Homer said.

"Are you trying to tell me something?" I asked.

"Maybe husbands wanted to be sure those jobs were always done and that they always had an ironed shirt at the ready," he said.

"You surely can't be saying that you think that wives should structure their lives like that today."

"Oh, no," he said. "But when I tried to find a golf shirt to put on this morning, I was wondering if you could see a Tuesday on your calendar in the days ahead."

CHAPTER 38

Ice House Houses Just That

Although summer, and haying, was about the busiest time on a ranch, Lynn had one annual job that was done in the coldest part of winter: cutting and putting up ice.

One first had to build an ice house, and Lynn built ours. It was about 12 square feet and made from small logs or poles about eight inches in diameter. The little junipers on the ranch filled that need. A supply of sawdust then was hauled from a nearby mill to insulate the giant cubes of ice.

An extended freezing period was required before Lynn and the other ranchers could put up their ice supply. It was harvested from the John Day River after it had frozen about a foot thick. Working in teams, the men used a cross-cut saw, and blocks were sawed from the ice, stacked in a wagon and hauled by team to the ice house.

We had no refrigerator, and ice in the ice house, which lasted well into the summer, enabled us to make hand-cranked ice cream on the Fourth of July and drink iced lemonade and ice tea, when there had been no relief from the heat for days.

Harvesting the ice had to be timed as critically as cutting the hay. It wasn't a job that permitted procrastination. If a Chinook wind moved in, the ice could start breaking up and go out in a hurry.

This heavy ice on the John Day sometimes created problems. In the spring when it went out, it might pile up in the river bed and along the banks and cause serious flooding. Our neighbor Mattie Stubblefield remembered one such incident when the ice went out on the John Day about half a century before.

It was late winter on the North Fork of the John Day and Jess Hyke, a rancher who lived along the river north of Monument, had been riding for cattle most of the day.

It was a disagreeable day. The chill of that Grant County winter had been worse than most. Jess, as he urged his horse forward a little faster, noted the depth of the ice on the river. There was no sign of its melting or breaking up although he'd heard there had been a thaw farther up the north fork.

"Sure no sign of it here," he mused.

A few minutes later Jess reined his horse to a stop. He strained to hear more clearly a strange rumbling sound coming from upriver. He held his breath to better listen to the unfamiliar sound.

"Maybe just wind in the pines," he decided. "But I never heard it sound like that before."

He urged his horse forward and was rounding a curve on the river when he heard the sound again — this time more distinctly.

He glanced up, following the frozen surface of the river back to its most distant point. The movement of something unusual caught his eye. He spurred his horse from behind a willow to have a better view upriver and for a moment he was unable to believe what he saw.

Moving slowly and ponderously down the bed of the John Day was a grayish-white wall some 20 feet high. It crept forward like a pallid monster, paying no heed to the water dammed up behind, or the river bank beside it. It moved inexorably, taking out whatever came in its path.

It took Jess a moment to understand the meaning of that vast wall. Then the significance came. That ice, and the water dammed behind it, might take out half of the ranches along the river, including his own. It might do great damage in the town of Monument and take out the bridge there. It could drown stock, even take lives.

Jess Hyke wheeled his horse around, gave it the spurs. He had to get back to his ranch to warn his wife, Ruby, and get word to town.

There was little else that could be done. Dynamiting sometimes broke up ice jams, but there was no time for that now.

John Williams was in the post office at Monument when word reached town that a 20-foot wall of ice was coming down river. The ice dam had reached the Oscar Schafer place some four miles north.

Williams lived with his daughter Mattie Stubblefield and her husband, Murd, at their ranch a little more than a mile from Monument. The house was a good 100 yards from the river in the summer, but it was hard to tell whether that would be enough now. John hustled home to spread the warning. It was good that he did. Water was a foot deep in the Stubblefield house before the ice went out. Bedding and other belongings were piled high on the furniture to keep it dry.

No lives were lost when the ice went out, but considerable damage was done. Huge chunks of ice, yards long and three feet deep, lay in the fields for days as evidence of the monster that had passed that way.

Many cattle were lost. They lay along the river, some drowned by breaking through the ice while trying to get water.

But just a few months later, people in Monument blessed that ice that had threatened homes, cattle and crops.

In April, Murd Stubblefield had spotted fever and was running a high temperature. Bill Hamilton, proprietor of a general mercantile store in Monument, sent ice from his ice house so Murd could have relief from his fever.

There are no ice harvests anymore, but some of the old ice houses on those ranches are silent reminders of an era now past — when refrigerators were a luxury that ranchers during the Depression could not afford.

CHAPTER 39

Learning to Cope with Hospitality

As an eastern Oregon rancher's wife 60 or 70 years ago I would have been a dud. My hospitality would never have passed muster.

There were numerous unwritten codes of ranch life back then. You weren't supposed to ask a rancher how many cattle he owned. You might as well ask him how much money he had in the bank — and most of them probably had none. The hospitality rule required that regardless of the hour, day or night, any visitor passing by should be invited to partake of a meal.

When George Cooper arrived at the gate after the noon meal was done and the dishtowel hung out to dry, a ranch wife was expected to ask if she could fix him something to eat. Her morale must have sunk lower than her shoes when Cooper replied, "Don't mind if you do."

To be fair, Cooper probably didn't plan it that way. He might have lived down on the river, but had land up north of Johnny Cake where he ran cattle in the summer. It would have been difficult for him to precisely plan his schedule since the cattle set the hours in a rancher's life.

The rancher's wife had to cook each meal from scratch. There were no microwave ovens back then and Cooper wouldn't have been content with a cheese sandwich.

So, not wanting to disgrace the hospitality of the ranch, the wife restarted the fire in the cookstove and peeled potatoes to fry or to boil (which she perhaps had to go to the garden and dig). She cooked venison in a pan with a bit of bacon fat and brewed a fresh pot of coffee. Then she anxiously watched the clock as the afternoon wore on and Cooper and her husband endlessly talked, and she tried to assess if Cooper would be there for the evening meal — referred to by us as supper.

Although the cattle might not let a rider time perfectly when he passed our place, my mother insisted there were acquaintances who timed their arrival at our ranch in order to partake of a meal if they were within 10 miles.

When unexpected visitors arrived to share a meal, it could be embarrassing. It seemed they always arrived when a rancher's wife was serving the skimpiest most unappetizing meal she'd put on the table in a long time.

Nor was it just single horseback riders who caused a ranch wife distress. The entire Kennedy family might arrive via wagon because Joe Kennedy had run out of binder twine and had come over to borrow some of ours.

Kennedy's wife and three children would pile out of the wagon while he explained, "Mary Sue and the kids decided they'd like to come along and visit for a while."

My Mother then nervously started watching the clock. Would they head for home before dinner? Not likely. It was more apt to be an all-day visit. Ranchers and their families liked to catch up on socializing every chance they got, so Mother had a pretty good idea she'd better think about putting on five extra plates for her noon meal.

Back then people socialized and visited in a slapdash way that I would have found stressful.

But even if that hospitality wasn't repaid formally, you knew sooner or later you'd be repaid in full. A party-line call might come from Cooper advising that our cow was over in his field again, but that it shouldn't be any problem for him to bring it over next day because he had to ride up to Johnny Cake. If my stepfather needed help for a couple of days with haying and wanted to borrow a harrow or a rake he had only to give Cooper a ring.

That reciprocal neighborliness and hospitality was a wonderful thing -- especially when unexpected visitors had to leave before mealtime.

CHAPTER 40

Playing with Smoke, Not Fire

Growing up in eastern Oregon, we kids were not wild, but we gave it a try.

When it came to cigarettes, none of us girls smoked. The primary reason, perhaps, was that we had no money with which to buy cigarettes. Boys pilfered their dad's smokes when their dads weren't looking and took them out behind the bar to give them a try, being careful not to set the barn on fire.

We girls didn't do that,

And some of the older high school boys smoked cigarettes in public, bought by money from working in the hayfields — if they couldn't sneak them from their dad.

For those of us nonsmokers, there was a substitute. It grew on our ranch: wild ivy. That wild ivy was a giant of a bush, comparable in size to the chokecherries and thorn apples that grew in little groves on the ranch. We were never sure that wild ivy was its correct name, but that was our designation for it. The stems of this wild ivy were hollow, so that if a piece of the stem, about the length of a cigarette, were cut from the bush and one end of that stick persuaded to burn after much effort, one could then draw smoke through the stick.

Feeling as daring as "Peck's Bad Boy," there I'd be beneath the wild ivy bush, a good mile or so from the ranch house so Mother could not monitor my efforts, giving smoking a good try.

It took a mighty effort to draw air through the passageways of the ivy stem, and my goal was to blow smoke rings. I never succeeded in creating smoke rings, and the amount of smoke I could draw from the stem was far less than one's halo of breath on a frosty winter day.

I was never sure whether smoking ivy constituted an immoral act, but I did not ask Mother, to find out.

In addition to possible immorality, something else bothered me about smoking the ivy. On our ranch, we kids were schooled in the dangers of poison oak and could readily identify it. Always, too, we heard about poison ivy, although no lessons were forthcoming with regard to it, When I sneaked to the wild ivy bush to give it a try, always I wondered if this might be real poison ivy and that I would show up on the morrow with telltale rash and sores around my mouth for this improper deed.

In retrospect, I am beholden to wild ivy. It dissuaded me from smoking cigarettes and made me wonder why one would want to. For that I have forever been grateful. How smart that wild ivy bush was.

Something else that I tried while hiking around the ranch — not immoral, but experimental — was chewing gum from the pine trees. Some friends, more knowledgeable than I in the ways of eastern Oregon, could readily tell what constituted satisfactory pine chewing gum. This "gum" consisted of little globules that formed on the bark and looked somewhat like pitch. I tried it a time or two, but rated it a sorry substitute for Wrigley's. Along with smoking wild ivy, I gave up chewing pine gum.

Nor did many high schoolers in Monument drink liquor, but stories circulated round our school regarding a few exceptions. A teenager who had a car, gas and money in his pocket, could drive the 60 miles to John Day, where a "moonshiner" from his home on the dark outskirts of town, sold liquor to kids — and all other comers. Anyone who went to that door — a person of any age — needed only to know the location of the house, knock at the door even in the dead of night, utter the right password and, for payment therewith, receive a jar of homemade moonshine.

Although there was no known liquor source in Monument, there seemed an abundance of liquor at every dance. For a time the State Police stationed in John Day, in order to be on hand for any disturbance, attended nearly every dance in Monument as faithfully as did we localites.

Liquor wasn't entirely an unknown at our ranch. My parents kept a bottle of whiskey for two purposes. If one of the family was stricken with a bad cold, flu, or respiratory ailment, we were dosed with a hot toddy, viewed as having almost magical powers. I seldom had such illnesses, so my experience with whiskey was scant.

A second reason for keeping whiskey was for animal medication. During lambing, if it turned cold, a just-born lamb could quickly freeze to death. When an inert lamb was discovered, as Lynn made the rounds during lambing, the lamb was brought to the ranch house, placed on a gunny sack on the open oven door where heat could warm it, and a big shot of the medicinal whiskey poured down its throat. Usually, the little lamb would begin to jerk with life shortly thereafter.

We had two kinds of "wild life" as kids in eastern Oregon. We sometimes stole watermelon. We did not regard that as a felony but rather as a rite of passage, a rite accepted more or less readily by the ranchers who grew the watermelons.

More daring than the stealing of watermelon — and not done as frequently — was the stealing of chickens. The chickens were not stolen with the idea of going into the poultry business but rather for the purpose of having a "chicken feed."

On one occasion, such a chicken feed was at our house. My parents had gone to spend several days at the ranch up the river, leaving me alone on our ranch near Monument. One evening, a bunch of us, for entertainment, decided on a chicken feed. Since our ranch was a considerable distance from any other ranch, I suggested that the chicken come from my Mother's chicken house. The boys in the group duly selected and killed the fowl that was brought to the house, picked and cleaned. A fire was built in the cookstove, the chicken was cooked and we then feasted. I was much concerned that Mother would notice that one of her chickens was missing and instead of attributing it to a coyote, interrogate her daughter.

Looking back, I don't know of any boy or girl in our high school who was ever arrested or charged with any crime. And that was a wonderful record. Today, we hear the sad stories of those whose lives have been ruined by drugs, and I think how fortunate we kids were that drugs were not a known substance when we were growing up. I do not think that any of my classmates would have become drug users, but we wanted to try things — just once — experience everything. That "just once" could have changed our lives.

How lucky we kids were to grow up in an era when smoking ivy was a bad thing. I wonder if an answer to all this today might be a wild ivy bush planted in every back yard.

CHAPTER 41

Endangered Experiences

Americans seem much interested in not wanting to lose any of our species — such as the spotted owl or plovers.

But Americans don't seem to mind the loss of experiences of the past — such as driving a horse and buggy, or going to an outhouse equipped with a catalog, or playing a pickup game of baseball on the sandlot on a summer evening — or the experience of milking a cow.

Almost every family — even those living in little towns — once had a milk cow or two. And every day of the year someone in the family headed out twice a day to milk them.

On our ranch, we always had a couple of milk cows. Each had its name and Daisy was our standby. She kept us in milk for years — except for a few periods in between when she decided enough was enough.

Every morning when she'd see the milker, with milk bucket in hand, heading for the barn, she'd moo, "good morning." That might not have been because she was glad to see the milker but because she was going to be reunited with her calf — and she expected a handout of hay.

Despite generally amicable relations between Daisy and the milker, there were definite rifts in that relationship at times.

Depending on who was doing the milking — and Daisy's mood — there were days when she didn't wish to part with her milk. Daisy was picky about the person who milked her. If you'd never milked before, Daisy knew — immediately — and displayed her disapproval. She swiveled her head around to look at that person hunched down beside her and even her bovine face could express disbelief.

A good milker was one who hunkered down beside the cow with milk bucket between his knees, and when he went to work, a steady stream of milk came forth so that foam appeared atop. It was a different matter with an inept milker. The attempt went on and on — much to Daisy's disgust — with only two or three inches showing in the bottom of the pail.

Daisy's tendency to not let down her milk was mostly avoided on our ranch because we turned in her calf when we started milking — not a practice on large commercial dairies. And some eastern Oregon ranchers took the cow's entire output, separated the milk, shipped the cream for cash — which was always in short supply — and fed the calf the skimmed product. This made feeding the calf more laborious. In our case, we opted to let the calf share the milking with us.

Understandably, this made Daisy and her calf happy. But although Daisy could control whether she let down her milk, she could not control the amount of milk that came from each of her outlets. I'm sure that Daisy would have been most happy to turn off milk supply to those outlets being appropriated by us humans trying to fill the milk bucket, and instead direct all output to outlets being used by the calf.

Since such was not the case, it was a contest between calf and human as to who would get the greater share.

If one wasn't a proficient milker, the calf won.

Competing against that calf could pose another problem. If the rambunctious little fellow didn't think it was getting its share, or that mama was not forthcoming rapidly enough with output, it butted Daisy in an impatient manner. If the milker's hand chanced to come into contact with that calf's determined "butting," the milker often left the corral with bloody knuckles.

If Daisy were feeling particularly contentious, she might express her displeasure in another way — with wicked kicks. If she were in need of Bag Balm, the danger was great and it could be a long morning for the milker — and probably even longer for Daisy.

Usually, the milker used a small stool to sit on — the better to beg enough milk from Daisy for the needs of our family. Some people, if they were young, could squat beside the cow and do the milking, but those with creaky knees, rebellious back, or hurting hips used a stool. The problem was that sitting on the stool slowed down reaction time if Daisy kicked. Her kicking presented two perils. First, if the milker were unable to get out of the line of that kick, the results could be painful. Second the bucket of milk could be in the way of that kick. And it was disgraceful to go back to ranch house with empty pail.

Maybe the best part of milking was when one headed back to the ranch house with full bucket of warm milk, leaving Daisy disgruntled because her calf hadn't gotten its share and the calf vowing it would get even on the next round by leaving the milker with bruised knuckles.

But there was a satisfaction heading toward the ranch house with that full pail — somewhat like picking berries and heading home with buckets filled. Then, too, there was the satisfaction that milking was over — for 12 hours. Milking was like the sun coming up and going down, twice a day regardless.

Milking machines have pretty much replaced humans as milkers, and those who have never milked a cow probably think that is of little consequence. The tragedy is that they will never have had the opportunity to experience the milking of a cow.

CHAPTER 42

Ranch Life Taught Gun Safety

We were anything but a warring people on our eastern Oregon ranch, but we had guns.

Guns were as necessary as shoes.

Our home had two guns: the utilitarian kind found on most ranches. We had no fancy pearl-handled pistols that cost as much as a diamond ring. Nor did we go to the dump to shoot at soup cans. Target practice wasn't necessary on the ranch. My stepfather, a fine shot, wasted a shell only if he thought he'd knocked his gun-sight askew. Target shooting smacked of playing with guns and, to my parents, guns were not toys.

The guns on our ranch included a .22 rifle used by everyone in our family when judged to be old enough. The second gun was my stepfather's Savage .30/.30 — touched by no one except Lynn. That gun was big-time stuff for things such as deer, elk — and heaven forbid — a horse or cow, if because of an accident or health problem, one had to be killed.

Lynn's rifle probably had killed as many deer as any gun in Grant County. Its sight was canted, its stock taped. He cut off part of the barrel. A superb shot at moving game, he knew the idiosyncrasies of his gun. He wasted no ammunition. One shot usually was sufficient.

We kids had scant training with regard to gun safety. We absorbed it by daily contact.

Whoever was assigned to take the .22 to kill a chicken for Sunday dinner did not have to be reminded to not shoot toward the house. If the chicken took up refuge between the rifle carrier and the house, the stalker patiently inveigled the chicken into a position so no cow, horse, other livestock or poultry were in the intended victim's whereabouts. If a chicken, perhaps suspecting that he was being stalked, took refuge behind a dense sagebrush, we did not presume there was nothing but the chicken behind that shelter. Nor did we countenance "sound shots." We had to know exactly what we were shooting at.

We were scared to death of the hunters who came from the "Valley" each fall to go hunting with Lynn. Some of those mighty hunters, we knew, took "sound shots" or they forgot, in the excitement of the chase, that a hunting partner was ahead of them in the path if a buck popped up on the horizon.

Guns in our house were never left loaded. We had great respect for guns and unbounded respect for loaded guns. When we carried guns and were with others, walking down a path, no gun barrel was ever pointed ahead. We never let the tip of the barrel rest on the ground, inadvertently causing the barrel to clog. We did not carry a gun with our finger on the trigger. Our guns, on the kitchen wall were handy. They weren't for burglars or bad men. Our doors were never locked — even when we were gone for days up at the other ranch. Burglars could have helped themselves to our guns if we had not taken them along, but for the most part, guns went everywhere we went.

Our chickens, despite sometimes being depleted in number by our .22 rifle, also benefited from it. Chicken hawks were numerous in Grant County and they hunted Mother's chickens hungrily. The chickens' effective warning system immediately alerted us to their presence. We then dashed for the .22 and took aim at the marauder. We did not often hit those overhead hawks, but it scared them away, much to the relief of the chickens.

We marveled at the instincts of these domestic fowl. We wondered if their mamas taught them about hawks so that even when they saw the shadow on the ground of one flying overhead, they sought cover. Or had they seen a fellow chicken struck down by a hawk? Or centuries and centuries ago, for their preservation, was this instinct provided?

Mother did not grow up around guns and knew not of their necessity until moving to eastern Oregon. She perhaps was the worst shot in Grant County despite casual instruction from Lynn about which eye to close when sighting. We chided Mother by saying that whatever she shot at was perfectly safe and used the example of the roving coyote as an example.

One day when Lynn was out in the field, she saw, trotting across the clearing below the house, a large coyote. Coyotes decimated our lamb population and our fowl. Mother hustled into the kitchen, took down the .22, hurried out, took careful aim and fired. She shot several more times, but the coyote did not fall to the ground. He did, however, stop and turn around, as if to look in amazement at how inept that shooter could be.

Although we did not regard guns as toys or playthings, eastern Oregon parents had no objection to their kids "playing guns."

The favorite toys of my little brother Jack were guns and knives. His favorite game: cowboys and Indians — almost the only game that he and his friends played. Jack had an arsenal of guns equaled by none. Any likely piece of wood or stick of kindling, as if with a wave of a wand, became a six shooter that never had to be reloaded by this cowboy who was taming the Wild West.

As he became older, he carved crude guns — always rifles. Every gun to him was as precious as that of a paper doll in a little girl's collection. If Mother made the mistake of not recognizing one of these sticks as a gun and putting it in the stove, it was a sad day for Jack — and for Mother. As girls outgrow dolls, Jack outgrew that stage and guns for him ceased to be playthings.

Today, in our house, Homer and I have secreted away, a .22 pistol. That's fine with me. I feel comfortable handling that gun and I'm grateful for that training in eastern Oregon where real guns were not toys.

CHAPTER 43

Easter Egg Hunts Daily
Event on the Ranch

Gathering eggs on our ranch was about as much fun as an Easter egg hunt
— except that our eggs were all either brown or white.

Mother didn't much care what color eggs her hens laid. She just wanted
production all year long. If her hens intermittently laid so many eggs that
she couldn't use them, then all took a vacation, she was upset with her
flock.

Our chickens had no pedigree or personality. They were the only living things on our ranch that we couldn't distinguish one from another.
Our sheep had faces as distinctive as people, and some we named after the
humans they looked like. Every dog, horse, cow and cat was named to fit its
personality — and improve communications. When I was sent out to the
pasture to bring in Bubbles, we all knew which horse I was to bring back.

None of our chickens had names. But Mother, in her attempt to provide us with year-round eggs, had several varieties of fowl, including leg-
horns, a grey-and-white mottled variety; and Minorca's, all black.

Although Mother had no more fondness for one hen than another, a
distinguishing characteristic, in her estimation, was the redness of the hen's
comb. She told us that a hen with a bright red comb was a "laying hen."

Woe to those hens whose combs became a wan pink. She thought of
chicken and dumplings when assessing them.

I not only liked to gather the eggs, I liked to feed the chickens their
two meals a day. Our chickens received no gourmet rations packed with

vitamins and minerals. Their feed was wheat: exact quantities measured in a lard bucket. Our chickens ate every kernel and thought it fine food. Although we rated chickens at the bottom of the intelligence scale in comparison to other creatures on our ranch, their intelligence served them well in one respect. Their mealtime sense was highly developed. They knew what "Come chick, chick, chick, chick" meant. And they weren't lazy. After eagerly gobbling up all visible grains of wheat, they scratched industriously in the dirt for over-looked kernels.

It gave me a sense of power to feed chickens. With lard pail in hand, I'd go to the feeding area near the chicken house. To alert those that weren't within sight, I sounded my "Come chick, chick, chick, chick," and all came running fast as ever their legs could carry them. The dispenser of feed had to sling handfuls over a large area so those at the bottom of the pecking order could partake.

The egg hunt came later in the day. And although I enjoyed gathering eggs, I hoped the hens at the chicken house would cooperate and obligingly hop off the nest when I approached. I disliked that prying them off the nest. It wasn't exactly that I was afraid of them, but all that flapping of wings, pecking and hopping around made me uneasy.

Mother tried to make it handy for those hens. She put up little wooden boxes in the chicken house, with straw in the bottom for nesting, and so the eggs wouldn't break. Sometimes, she put artificial eggs of china or glass in their nests. This was to make them feel as if their efforts were not all in vain and they really had laid an egg.

Seasonally, the hens took it into their heads to "set." And if Mother, the ruler, didn't deem it a proper time, that hen was banished to the "Bastille", a little pen with no nest. A couple of days in that solitude and the hen usually was ready to give up the idea.

Sometimes, though, the hens outfoxed Mother. They'd start a nest under a sagebrush or in the barn. When the hen accumulated a goodly number of eggs, she went about hatching them. Twenty-one days later, she'd make a proud appearance, with fuzzy little chicks scurrying behind, smiling triumphantly at Mother as if to say, "I told you so."

Even when they had no intention of setting, some hens laid their eggs in places other than the chicken house. Mother then would try to outthink the hens. Mostly those hens were braggarts, and each time they laid an egg they'd tell all of Grant County about it. Then, listening to the direction from which the announcement came, Mother detailed me to search that area. Sometimes I'd discover a well-hidden nest with perhaps a dozen eggs in it. That was better than an Easter egg hunt because never on Easter did I find a quantity of eggs in one spot.

Mother's chickens were important to her. Eggs were big on our menu — a necessity for breakfast and for baking. The young roosters were designated "fryers." Chickens not knowing how to play the game ended up in the chicken and noodle pot. Sometimes, Mother's chickens even provided a cash crop. When she had a surplus of eggs, they were traded in on our grocery bill at Boyer's Cash Grocery.

I miss hearing roosters crow, except that they often alarmed one that it was almost time to get up. But it seems to me that nature made a mistake. Roosters don't have so much to crow about. It's the hen that lays the egg.

CHAPTER 44

That Was Entertainment

Camaraderie made up for what we lacked in culture when I was growing up in Monument.

We had no concerts, opera, lectures. We high school kids had no movies, skating rink. Not even an ice cream parlor where we could perch on high stools and talk about our latest crush, which would not have taken long. Only about a dozen boys were in our school.

Monument's cultural events of the year were our high school plays. The teacher whose chore it was to produce these programs must have looked over available talent with misgivings, her principal pleasure being when it was over.

The entertainment included a three-act play and some sort of performance between acts. Our plays were not of the dramatic type. No "Romeo and Juliet" in Monument. Our teacher-director hoped for comedies that would fulfill that humorous purpose. It was hard to find a suitable play with a cast not exceeding the number of students willing to take part. Some of the big, burly boys who rode horses to school and wore black cowboy hats to dances, would rather have been bucked from a horse than to walk onto the stage.

We had no tryouts for our productions. Our teacher was grateful for willing participants and, as soon as a date was set, we put up hand-lettered posters: one for the post office, one for Boyer's Cash Grocery, one for Gabler's Garage. Our production was always a Saturday one-time show. It took the entire countryside to fill our auditorium for one night.

For several weeks before the program, we practiced at night — no doubt an annoyance for the teacher, but we kids liked being out — even though it meant walking the mile or two home after school, eating supper and then walking the round-trip back to school after dark.

Our between-act entertainment was even harder for our teacher-director to provide. Monument had no piano, dance, vocal or music teacher. What our director did manage was a quartet of us girls. Few boys in our high school wanted to sing "Blue Hawaii" with the girls.

Our musical between-act renditions varied considerably with the teacher. Those teachers who had grown up in cattle country chose "Drifting Along with the Tumbling Tumbleweeds" and the little-doggies-going-to-Wyoming-to-make-a-new-home type of song. Teachers who came from the "outside" chose a more cultural tack with such as "The World is Waiting for the Sunrise."

But then our teacher one year had another between-act choice. A new girl came to school: the stepdaughter of a long-single rancher. Betsy was raised in the city. She'd had tap-dancing lessons and was willing to teach some of us girls her dance routines. We ordered black patent tap shoes that tied on with a bow. Our mothers made matching long-sleeved satin blouses and black sateen shorts and onto the stage we pranced. Monument had never seen tap dancers before. Nor perhaps did they wish to see us again. But we were caught up with Ginger Rogers fever and added to our repertoire. For our next between-act performance, we devised a "fan dance" and put up posters advertising our act. Our community buzzed. What was Monument coming to? Our only minister, a part-time volunteer, announced boycott of the performance — visualizing no doubt the Sally Rand variety of dance.

Our audience that evening must surely have been disappointed when we danced onto the stage in old-fashioned long skirts and decorously hid our faces behind fans.

For our plays, costumes and props were minimal, although on one occasion we did ourselves proud. That play opened during a rainy thunder-and-lightning storm. Backstage, we kids bent a flexible metal sheet to emit a noise somewhat like thunder, poured buckets of water into tubs to simulate rain, and turned flashlights toward the stage for "pretend" lightning.

Dress rehearsal was a night or two before the "big night" after which our teacher-director must surely have been in despair. We kids forgot our lines. When an actor delivered the line, "Oh, here comes Penelope," Penelope, having fun backstage, did not show up.

We went home from dress rehearsal disheartened. But on the big night, adrenaline flowed, heightened by stage fright. The auditorium began to fill. Ranch families came from Top, Kimberly, Courtrock, up Rudeo, even from Long Creek and Spray. Perhaps not so much because of our play but because a community dance would follow.

There were the usual gaffes. Harrington goes to answer the phone, but offstage the phone does not ring. Hortense does not render the line that is the cue for Bailey to come on stage, but the audience seems not to have known, or to particularly care.

And when the final curtain came down, although occasionally the recalcitrant curtain refused to do so, we listened to the applause, gauging its length and enthusiasm. We lapped up the praises about its being the best play in years, we kids thought a little about Hollywood, our teacher collapsed in exhaustion.

And the ranchers, who had not seen each other in quite a while, talked about the crops and the lack of rain. And the ranchers' wives talked about the latest recipe for seven-day sweet pickles and the young kids ran around like wild ponies until their moms corralled them.

It was no Oscar-winning performance. But in Monument, we didn't care. We had little culture, but we were rich in camaraderie.

CHAPTER 45

Grease Was the Word

Mother didn't save bits of twine all tied together into a big ball of string; she didn't make pajamas for me from flour sacks, but she was a devout and venerating saver of bacon fat.

She was the queen of bacon-fat savers. No dab of it was wasted in our household.

The accumulated bacon fat was kept in a container on the back of the kitchen range. The container had no cover, which facilitated the frequent addition or use of bacon drippings. That container was like sourdough starter: continually added to, continually used and never entirely used up. Although it was of no concern to me at the time, the age of that bacon fat at the bottom of that container makes for interesting surmise now.

Seldom did the bacon that furnished the bacon fat come from a store. Sometimes, we bought a slab from a neighbor who had hogs. Sometimes we raised our own. But my parents soon discovered that pigs can be a trouble-some kind of livestock to raise. Perhaps it was because we didn't keep our pigs penned up. They were not the immense hogs — so big they were scarcely mobile — such as seen at the state fair. Our pigs were the smaller, rangier variety that were imbued with wanderlust.

If our phone rang of a morning and Theo Owings, a neighboring ranch-er's wife, called to tell Mother that our pigs had shown up in their yard, which was a good two miles away, it was a rotten day for my Mother.

Lynn, my stepfather, was out in the field. Now Mother, as a recent transplant to an eastern Oregon ranch was in a dither. Did this housewife now saddle up her horse and go after a sow and five little piglets, round them up and persuade them to head home? Did she go out in the field and summon Lynn from his important timely harvest, or did she let our sow and five piglets root around in the neighbor's yard?

Regardless of the source of our bacon in those days, it was the big, thick, substantial kind and anything but lean—although these days, as humans seem to get more obese, today's pork gets more lean.

As the bacon fried in the big, black cast-iron skillet, the fat oozed out and bubbled around the slices, and that accumulation then was poured into the bacon fat container. No bacon fat in our home ever went to waste. It had a hundred uses.

When Mother cooked fresh green beans from the garden, she seasoned them with a bit of crisply cooked minced bacon, and seasoning of bacon fat.

She fried potatoes frequently, and before they were sliced into the heavy skillet, she first added a considerable quantity of bacon fat.

If she wanted to make gravy for a meal when she didn't have the kind of meat that provided gravy makings, she put a big quantity of bacon fat in the pan, added flour and let it brown before adding milk.

Mornings when she didn't cook bacon, our eggs were flavored with bacon fat.

Our biscuits knew about bacon fat, too. The pan in which they were baked first received a sizable quantity.

Perhaps it was in part because of the Depression that Mother saved bacon fat. She was a frugal homemaker. She had to be. The price of cattle was down, as was the price of wool from sheep. The hens stopped laying just when she was hoping to have a great surplus of eggs to apply to our grocery bill. But Mother, bacon fat queen, would have saved bacon fat if she had won the Lottery.

So it was that when Homer and I were first married, I adopted the same bacon-fat saving ritual. That was made easier because we were given an aluminum three-piece set with salt and pepper shakers and round container, with lid, imprinted "Bacon Drippings."

It sat on the back of the stove and, as did my Mother, I added all bacon fat to it. As I recall, patriotic citizens gave up their bacon fat and all other such waste fats for the war effort, but not the Rohses. Our bacon fat was added to the container on the back of the stove.

I used bacon fat for any number of things — learned from Mother.

But then there came a time when I began to have misgivings about saving bacon fat. We began even to have misgivings about bacon.

Fat became public ogre Number One. We heard about cholesterol, arteries clogged with fat, bodies hampered with accumulated obesity, and other such medical findings announced every day.

So the lonely little container sat on the back of the stove, and sometimes it would be weeks before I'd add anything to it— and as many weeks without my using anything from it. And then I did the unthinkable, I put my bacon drippings container in a garage sale, and some devout bacon-fat saver snatched it up.

Last week I said to Homer, "I'm hungry for bacon. Let's have bacon for breakfast tomorrow morning."

"Sounds good," he said.

We don't like little thin slices of bacon, but we found some good thick bacon in a deli, and we didn't fry it in a big black skillet. We arranged the slices on a little rack, put it in the microwave and the fat ran down into the grooves of the tray. In no time at all, the bacon was crisp, and I was careful to blot the bacon with a paper towel, carefully and thoroughly, so that no unnecessary trace of fat saturated the bacon we were to eat.

Homer took the little rack on which the bacon was cooked. "You don't want this bacon fat, do you?" he asked.

"I guess not," I said, and he poured all that good bacon fat into a can, and it went in the garbage.

I trust that my arteries, my cholesterol count and the scale with which I shall weigh myself tomorrow morning before eating anything will appreciate what I'm sacrificing for them.

I'm sorry that bacon fat, which my Mother taught me to religiously save, has come to such an end. But even though we're discarding bacon fat these days, I'd like it to know that I still consider it a good friend.

CHAPTER 46

When I Became a Buckaroo

Although it was the Depression era, we kids in eastern Oregon didn't dream of being rich when we grew up. We grew up wanting to be buckaroos. To be a buckaroo, you had to ride everything on the ranch, be it horses, cattle or mules. One didn't always stay on when one rode, but one attempted.

I was a late starter in acquiring horse savvy. We didn't move to eastern Oregon until I was 8, and before that I'd never even ridden a rocking horse.

In eastern Oregon, horses were part of our routine. We rode horses to town to get the mail and to get groceries. I rode them over to the Stubblefields when I went to see my friend, Reta. We rode them when we went after the cows. Before we had a tractor, horses powered the haying, plowing, disking and seeding machines.

In high school, we sometimes socialized on horseback. Half a dozen of us kids congregated to ride horses down to the dam on the John Day to go swimming at night.

My stepfather, Lynn, who grew up in eastern Oregon, knew all about horses, but he was too busy with chores to give riding lessons. So I watched him ride and noted how comfortable he looked—as if he were in his personal lounge chair. Good riders, I deduced, didn't dump themselves in the saddle and slump like a sack of flour with feet dangling out of stirrups. Lynn's back was straight; his reins at the ready, his horse held its head high and stepped out as briskly as if it were in a parade.

Just as we knew our horses, our horses knew each of us riders and assessed how much they could get away with. If Lynn was in the saddle, it was no play day. But when my sister, Mother or I got on a horse, they knew we were patsies and did all manner of undesirable tricks. As I rode down a trail, if Skinny saw a succulent tidbit growing five feet off the path, he meandered off to avail himself of that tender morsel despite my kicking him in the ribs and jerking the reins. Had Lynn been in the saddle, Skinny would not have dared to do such.

My goal wasn't so much to look good on a horse but rather to just stay on. Often we rode without a saddle, which makes that more difficult. A saddle, of course, is equipped with saddle horn and other appendages to which one can cling, although only a novice does so. The saddle also provides a step up onto the horse.

But at times it was too much bother to saddle a horse if one were only riding down to the pasture to bring in the cows or horses, so we rode bareback. When a horse was in a corral or barn at the ranch house we could lead it to the watering trough, or someone would give us a hand up so we could easily get astride that horse without saddle. But sometimes no horse was available when it was necessary to bring in the horses, and after walking out to find them in the pasture, it seemed only logical to ride one home bareback. The problem was that one first had to get on the horse's back—with no aids nearby. A horse, when you attempt to leap on it, looks as tall as the Washington Monument. One nevertheless makes a tremendous leap, hoping to throw one leg across its back while holding onto halter or bridle; hoping also that the horse stands patiently as one attempts to scramble aboard.

If there is a large rock, the side of a bank, a stump or a log, one can position the horse beside that to make the jump less difficult. This method can also be calamitous. I once led a horse to a sizable log, misjudged the height, made a mighty jump, cleared the horse's back by a considerable amount and landed on the other side.

Bubbles, another saddle horse that my Mother, sister and I sometimes rode, was not exactly wild, but that bay mare was flighty. Just when I had myself lolled into inalertness as we rode along a trail, she would leap four feet sideways at some supposed danger. When I rode her to town, I prayed that we would not meet a blaring truck or a speeding car along the main road. In one place, the road through a cut was so narrow it left no shoulder for Bubbles and me. Bubbles was afraid of cars and, although occasionally she steeled herself for such encounters when I talked calmingly to her, at other times she shied violently away from or toward the vehicle. When I rode Bubbles to town I was afraid we might end up as roadkill.

Bubbles had other foibles. She had a round belly. When we attempted to saddle her, she made even more of that belly. She had learned that by swelling her girth to larger proportions, the saddle cinch then was more comfortable, so with all her might she pooched out her belly until we had finished saddling her. Then, ready to mount, with foot in stirrup, we would notice that the cinch was so loose our saddle could easily have turned.

Bubbles' rotund build had another disadvantage. When I rode her bareback, Bubbles' Santa Claus belly caused my legs to stick out like the arms of a windmill. I presented no handsome sight when riding Bubbles bareback. Further, when I rode her bareback, she was disposed to trot so that with every bounce, there was blue sky between mount and me.

When I was sent to get the milk cows, as sun was disappearing behind West Gulch, I went afoot if no saddle horse was in the barn. Then, having found the cows, it seemed a shame to walk home when the cows were merely giving milk for their keep. Should they not also provide a ride? Some were too wild for me to ride home, but Sue, a mature Guernsey-like animal was my saddle cow. If she appeared in a tranquil mood and I could get close enough to get astride her broad round back, off we and the other cows would plod single file on the trail to the ranch house.

She was a pretty good saddle cow while following the trail through the sagebrush, but when she came to the large clearing around the house, old Sue had had enough. She wanted to play buckaroo. She broke into a lurching gallop, and agile as a calf, kicked up her hind legs and dumped me in the needlegrass,

Regardless of how an attempted ride ended, we kids in eastern Oregon wanted to be buckaroos. Of course, it was preferable to not get thrown off a horse or a cow, but it was better to have been displaced than never to have gotten on.

CHAPTER 47

For Love of the Game

In hand-me-down green and white uniforms minus Nike emblems, in mismatched tennies and socks, we Rimrock Savages took to the basketball court in Monument. Our games were about as unlike the basketball played by schools today as a pick-up game is unlike the Olympics.

For one thing, the number of people on our squad constituted a big difference. Monument High's enrollment was about 25. We were lucky to have a couple of subs on the bench.

Our harassed coach also served as high school principal and one of two teachers. We had no Rose Garden in which to perform and our school lacked a gym. Games were played in the community hall. That facility had no bleachers or rows of seats ascending so far into the heavens that binoculars were needed to see us players. Its only seats were a single row of benches around the perimeter of the floor and a bit of standing room for the males that held out in the far end of the hall.

At the other end of the building was the stage, where mothers tucked in their sleepy young ones during the game. But on basketball nights, little Monument rocked. The entire town — about 125 — and surrounding ranch families turned out to cheer us as enthusiastically as if it had been a Super Bowl contest.

When we took to the floor, our girls' basketball team was no Nike style show. It was good that our little community knew all players, since uniforms did not have individual names blazoned across the back. There was good reason for that: Uniforms were used season after season. When we players were handed a uniform, we hoped that in the past seasons someone of about the same size had been on the team. Otherwise, the "fit" of the uniform was anything but.

These two-piece uniforms were the extent of matched attire. Helen Gollyhorn's shoes might be of the high-topped black canvas variety, worn with black socks. My sister, Lillian, might be playing in low, white tennies and green half socks.

In that era, we gals did not have to be race horses to play basketball. Our court was divided into three sections. In the center section were the center and side-center. After each basket, the ball was brought back to center court, where the centers then jumped. At one end of the floor were the two forwards, and in the section at the other end, the two guards. We stayed on our one-third of the floor — not exactly a strenuous game.

Then, over the years, it was determined that women could be a bit more vigorous. The side-center position was eliminated and the center could run all over the floor, whereas the guards and forwards stayed in their halves. By the time I went to Lewis & Clark (then Albany College) and later to the University of Oregon, all five of us could dash all over the court at will — and everyone could shoot.

Monument's opponents were Spray, Long Creek, Dayville, perhaps Fossil, Mount Vernon, Prairie City or Mitchell, and also John Day. We trembled in our tennies when we played John Day. They were the big city team. Our adrenaline gushed when we went there.

We had no school buses to take us to games, so townspeople and parents took us in cars. The 60-mile trip to John Day necessitated having a restaurant meal before our evening game. And always our coach ordered for us: a poached egg on toast. With that as sustenance, we took to the floor.

Our team had no worries about being sanctioned because practices started too early. Our coach was probably lucky to have staged a few run-throughs before the first game — what with serving as principal, teacher, and perhaps staging one school drama, before basketball season began. So it was that our team was not exactly over-trained or overburdened by learning plays. My recollection is that we had one play, a simple one, that suited our team — except that we seldom remembered to put it into effect.

If, in a crucial game, the score was tied and the coach called a time-out, it was not so he could hurriedly detail a diagram for a winning play on the clipboard. He was probably more apt to be wringing his hands in frustration. But teams we competed against mostly were of the same ilk, which must have somewhat comforted our leader.

I have no memories of our Rimrock Savages girls' team ever participating in playoffs. Hopefully that was because there was no provision for girls' playoffs then.

Nor did Monument have cheerleaders in abbreviated costumes -- an omission hard to imagine in today's basketball scene. With Monument High's few students, we were lucky to mount both a boys' and a girls' team. Nor did it ever occur to one of us team players to turn toward the crowd and exhort them to cheer more loudly for us. Our team followers needed no urging. Their noise decibel was admirable. It rocked the community hall.

Since enrollment at Monument was insufficient for a boys' football team, basketball was our only team sport. In the spring, we played work-up softball for our own entertainment. Every spring we had track and went to John Day for the countywide track tournament.

Not even at Albany College or at Oregon did our girls' basketball team compete with other schools. At Albany, we played community teams from around Portland as part of the Portland parks and recreation program.

Our basketball team had no uniforms, nor did most of the other teams. Our Albany student body cared not the least about our team. No one came to cheer us on. We played for the love of playing.

At the University of Oregon, intramural games made up our entire program. No scholarships were available for women athletes, and we had never heard of a male college player being enticed with big money to leave school to play for a pro team.

But I doubt if players today who are paid millions of dollars a year to come out on the floor, enjoyed it any more than we.

Today, as we read about the players' tantrums, transgressions and egos, it makes one wonder if they have forgotten that fun is the name of the game.

CHAPTER 48

Our Summer Destination

We didn't have a lot of places to go to in eastern Oregon — but during the summer we could go to the garden.

We had a big garden. A fenced plot. A little oasis.

Early in the spring, my stepfather, Lynn, brought in the horses to plow the space. Then we waited impatiently for the weather — or the Farmer's Almanac — to advise that it was time for the seeding and planting. Then in went the peas, the carrots, radishes, leaf lettuce, beets. Seed potatoes were cut up and planted in hills. Tomato plants were set out. Within the week, Mother and Lynn made daily trips to the garden to see what was coming up.

Not until there was something edible in the garden did it have appeal for me. But as the days warmed in Grant County and the wild syringa bloomed and the needle grass turned dry and crackly, I became interested in it.

And one day at breakfast, Mother announced, "I think we may have a mess of peas in a day or two."

Not only was it a source of pride among the ranchers as to who produced the first peas, but who had the first leaf lettuce and radishes, The first tomato of the season was as prestigious as winning a blue ribbon for one's sheaf of wheat at the Grant County Fair.

It was then that I started going to the garden.

Sometimes it was because Mother sent me there to pick peas, pull carrots, or get leaf lettuce, but I went there, too, on my own because I found it an interesting place.

After Mother announced that there might soon be a picking of peas, I waited until she was occupied and then — surreptitiously — headed for the garden. I suspected Mother was looking forward to that first harvest of peas and that she would not appreciate my eating half of her crop. So I ate only a modest amount — hoping she would not miss them.

It was a little like an Easter egg hunt, rummaging among the pea vines to find pods big enough to have edible peas within. I liked the handy little openers that nature gave to peas: The handy hook with the string attached so that when you pulled on that little opener, it worked almost like a zipper. Within were the peas, like little pearls in an oyster. Sweet as candy. Tender as just-baked bread.

As the days warmed, the leaf lettuce and little radishes and carrots came on. When the carrots were only about as big as one's little finger, we began eating them — to thin the rows. To cook them, Mother scarcely scraped away their thin skin and on my visits to the garden I pulled the carrot, from the moist loamy soil, shook off the loose dirt, bit off the end of it, and with the leafy top as a handle, ate it straight-away.

Long before the beets were large enough on their own, we had beet greens with little beet nodules attached. Beet greens were a favorite — more so than spinach — although spinach from our garden was not to be turned down.

The rows in our garden did not feature exotic things: No artichokes, no Chinese cabbage, no eggplant, no kohlrabi. We didn't yet know about broccoli — and for some reason there was no zucchini in our plot. But our garden grew well what was planted and it piled our summer tables high. String beans, corn, cucumbers, cabbage and tomatoes were big in our garden. The tomato vines hung heavy with the big red orbs and I ate them in the garden — leaning forward so the juices missed my blouse. But although I adored the tomatoes, I parted the vines gingerly because of the huge puffy tomato worms — as long as a cigarette and bigger around than a man's finger — that often hid in the vines. As the tomatoes ripened, out came the canning jars. Like the squirrels, Mother was already thinking ahead to winter.

As the sun stayed long each day and toasted the earth, the cantaloupe and watermelon came on. Of a hot summer night, before bedtime, we sat on the porch eating watermelon — not with forks but with a big slab in hand. My sister and I had competition as to who was the longer watermelon-seed spitter. Had someone told us we would someday eat watermelon that had no seeds, we would have been dismayed.

But the garden by no means did it all, as ranchers' wives knew well. Before starting a meal, Mother had to dig the potatoes — robbing them from the hills, taking only the bigger ones and leaving the plant intact. Leaf lettuce had to be picked leaf by leaf. Peas had to not only be picked, but shelled. The beans had to be picked, the cabbage cut. The mature ears of Golden Bantam had to be found on the stalk. Then the big kettle went on the stove, with water enough to cover the ears — not just one ear apiece but perhaps a dozen for our meal.

The ground was good to us.

After we moved from the Monument ranch to the ranch up the John Day, the raspberry patch was our joy. Every morning Mother went to the garden to pick the sweet red fruit. Sometimes we ate raspberries three times a day: in sauce dishes, as wonderful raspberry cobbler, raspberry shortcake, raspberry jam.

But as the summer tired, so did our garden. Winter was a comin' in. The potatoes were dug, their withering vines cast aside. The big Hubbard squash, the winter cabbage, the onions big as a man's fist, went to the cellar.

And the spent garden became a stark, dismal almost funereal place that no one went near.

Perhaps we seemed disloyal to this benefactor that treated us so well during the summer, but in truth we were not. We, as well as our garden that now was drowsing in deserved rest, were already thinking of spring.

CHAPTER 49

Teakettles, Old Friends

In years past, the teakettle may not have been the heart of the home, but it was at least a lung, or a liver, or a kidney.

Ours — a permanent fixture on the ranch house cookstove — was no two-cup affair. Nor were ranch house teakettles the "whistling" kind that announced boiling water so shrilly one had to run from the kitchen. Ranch wives didn't rate those as "working" teakettles but more the "tea for two" type for the little old lady in the easy chair with the shawl across her knees.

Ours was a big heavy aluminum teakettle that held several quarts. Lacking hot water tank, that teakettle and the reservoir on our cookstove were our hot water system. The reservoir, on the far right side of our stove, held much more water than the teakettle, but it was a "plodder." Reservoir water was heated by radiant heat from the firebox, and the oven was between firebox and reservoir, so it was slow to heat. At best, the water in it was far from scalding.

Another problem with the reservoir was that it did not automatically refill itself. Buckets or big pans of water had to be dumped therein. That heated water was handy for washing one's hands or for dishwashing. But the dishwasher who used the reservoir water — my sister or me — was not mandated to fill the reservoir and seldom, if ever, did we do it voluntarily. So at the next dishwashing, hot reservoir water was usually not available. In such cases, the boiling water in the teakettle came to the aid.

It held not enough to fill the dishpan, but when cold water was added, a dishwasher could get by — and it was better than waiting for a dishpan of water to heat on the stove.

We blessed our teakettle often. On cold winter nights we were grateful when it provided hot water for washing our face before going to bed. If one found the reservoir empty, the teakettle saved the day. Even if the fire in the stove had been out for a couple of hours, the teakettle water was hot, and a cup or two was far better than cold water straight from the spring.

During the day, the tea kettle was Mother's helper countless times. If she was late with supper and feared the potatoes would never boil she started them with boiling water from the teakettle.

If one of us kids came in with cut or skinned knee, she cleansed it with hot water from the teakettle — before applying the inevitable Mercurochrome or iodine, and flour-sack bandage.

When summer came and the tomatoes ripened, she picked big pans of them and poured boiling teakettle water over them and the skins slid off like banana peels. When she canned peaches, the willing teakettle easily slipped off those furry skins.

Lynn, my stepfather, did not often shave, but when Mother's exhortations moved him to do so, the teakettle was his friend. His shaving brush sat in a little cup of shaving soap in the medicine cabinet in the kitchen. His razor strop hung on the kitchen wall. His straight-edge razor was slapped back and forth on the strop for a sharper edge. He poured teakettle water into the enamelware washbasin and in it swished his brush, then into the soap — and plopped it on his face until he looked as if he'd grown a white Santa Claus beard. Hot water made the job more acceptable.

And the teakettle was a godsend when Mother cooked chicken.

Chicken wasn't then bought defeathered, deskinned, deboned, frozen and available in neat packages of your choice of wings, legs, breast or thighs. Our chickens arrived in the kitchen still warm from the kill — and Mother fervently hoped she wasn't the one who had to kill it. If Lynn was at the house, she petitioned him. A fine shot, he usually killed the designated chicken with the .22 rifle. I was alternate chicken killer, but Mother was never totally sure of my skill as a marksman and it was vital that an accurate marksman undertake that job. That marksman aimed at the chicken's head — a small target. And although the chicken's body represented a much bigger target, that was the last thing Mother wanted. A shot in the body ruined much of the meat and made it difficult to prepare for cooking. But despite the possibility of the marksman missing his target, Mother much preferred shooting the chicken to killing it by chopping off its head.

If this method were used, we kids were employed to "corner" or "herd" the designated chicken into a corner, or into the chicken house. Lynn then grabbed it by its legs — its head dangling down and craning around to figure out what terrible happening was in store. At the chopping block in the woodshed, Lynn cut off its head with the axe, swiftly and hopefully painlessly.

Being executioner in this manner was the last thing that Mother wanted to do. If Lynn were gone, she dubiously looked to me. My problem was that I was not really big enough to wield the axe. The chicken had to be held on the block with one arm, while lifting the axe with the other. One had to be strong enough to accurately and finally accomplish the act. If one missed and hit the chicken a glancing blow, it was not a good day.

After the kill, the teakettle came into play. It was vital for defeathering the chicken. This was facilitated by placing the chicken in the dishpan and pouring over it a teakettle of boiling water — thereby making it easier to pull out the feathers without tearing the flesh. Picking the chicken was an even more laborious job if pinfeathers had to be removed. The chicken then still had to be cleaned.

Looking back one wonders why chicken was in the pot every Sunday. But for farmers and ranchers there was no other way.

Nowadays, teakettle manufacturers must have a hard time. Teakettles seldom are seen on kitchen stoves these days. Not every kitchen even has a teakettle. Hot water comes from hot water pipes, or the micro boils it in seconds.

Before that came about, those teakettles were important. Our faithful teakettle was a staunch old friend.

CHAPTER 50

Confessing the Sins of Childhood

The statute of limitations has run out. It is time to reveal the crimes of my youth, although I'm not sure what the official criminal charge would have been — perhaps petty larceny or minor theft.

But had I been summoned before a judge, I would have pleaded "Not guilty." Not guilty because in eastern Oregon my crime was regarded as universal summer entertainment. We kids stole watermelons.

It was really the fault of our elders. As far back as anyone could remember, kids around Monument traditionally stole melons from the fields. It was not because of passion for watermelon but because it was the traditional thing to do.

Once or twice during the summer, a bunch of us kids on a Saturday night would get together on horseback (watermelon thieves didn't usually have cars).

We had our favorite people to steal from — not because their melons were sweeter but because it was no fun to steal from jolly John Caruthers and his nice wife, Molly. And certainly we wouldn't steal from the Gordons, who had 11 kids and could use every melon they raised. Instead we chose to raid the patch of someone like Ernest Hedges. Rumor had it that he kept a shotgun by his bed. We didn't really think he'd shoot at us, but it added to the excitement.

And one story, that long had circulated in Monument about a young man who was shot to death stealing watermelons, always was in the back of our minds. On Memorial Day, we made a habit of visiting his gravemarker when we went to the cemetery to remember that sorry chapter in our town's history. But, if historians are correct, the shooting had more to do with bad blood between two families than with stealing watermelons.

Watermelon stealing was not a daylight crime. As we waited for dusk on summer evenings we had considerable time to plan our theft.

Often as many as a dozen of us congregated and Ernest's was almost always our first choice. His patch was a considerable distance from his house and was fenced with barbed wire.

When it was finally dark, we'd ride down the trail toward Ernest's house. If one of the kids was scared, or couldn't run very fast, he'd hold the horses' reins and stay with them trying to keep them quiet while the rest of us invaded the patch.

Stealthily we'd crawl through the first barbed wire fence, creep carefully across the field and cautiously crawl through the fence adjacent the patch. We were afraid to use flashlights or lanterns for fear of being seen.

In the dark it was a problem to find large melons and to tell ripe from green. The biggest boys made the selection because they'd be carrying the loot.

Before we'd been in the patch more than a few minutes, some nervous thief would be certain he heard Ernest coming with shotgun. We'd run pell-mell, rushing out of the patch in the dark. The boys carrying the watermelons looked pregnant in the sparse light of the stars, wobbling along fast as they could with 2-foot long watermelons in their arms.

In our haste, someone was sure to get hung up on the barbed wire, but as we fled the scene it was every thief for himself. If you were hung up, it was up to you to get unsnagged.

Back with our horses, we hurriedly clambered astride, riding at full speed up the trail to our designated meeting place along the John Day River to enjoy our watermelon feast.

It wasn't that we were hungry for them. All of us probably had big watermelon patches in the gardens at home, but even green stolen watermelon tastes good.

No theft should be condoned, so I no doubt rationalize when I suggest that the old-time custom of stealing watermelons might have merit. That was one way we kids were entertained. And lawless though it was, it was far better than the entertainment seekers who smoke pot today.

CHAPTER 51

Preserving Childhood Lessons

On days when Mother canned, I wished I were somewhere else.

Mother probably wished she were somewhere else, too, but in those days all good housewives canned. Canning was our means of preserving food — although home economists would have shuddered at the open-kettle method Mother used.

On canning day, our kitchen became a processing plant. Steam wafted up from the dishpan of boiling jars on the wood stove. The big kettle of fruit bubbled away. A saucepan of hot water was at the ready for the little round flats with the sticky edges.

Canning days started badly when Mother gave me my first assignment: bringing up empty fruit jars from the cellar. I disliked our dark, spooky cellar, especially when assigned to bring up empty fruit jars.

Unlike rushing down to get a squash or potatoes and hurrying back up the dirt steps, gathering fruit jars took time: two dozen quart jars, three dozen of the two-quarts. The empty jars were at the back of the wide shelves and our cellar had no lights. Each time I reached to the back of the shelf I feared I would touch some living thing or stick my hand into a spider web.

I was the menial helper on canning day, and canning offered no cease of menial tasks. The big boxes of apples on the back porch served notice that this was a day when I would have not a minute to myself. After Mother quality control-checked the jars by running her finger around the top edge to discover nicks or chips, I became jar washer.

Only two things about washing jars had appeal. What was in the bottom of the unwashed jars sometimes was interesting. Mostly our flats were inadvertently thrown away as fruit was opened, so jars were stored only with metal ring atop. Often in the bottom of those jars were interesting assortments of dead spiders and other insects — some unrecognizable — but I would not have been surprised at anything found in those jars that came from the cellar.

The other entertaining part of washing jars was to see if I could get my hand entirely inside the jars. My left hand went in more easily than my larger right hand. This byplay aggravated Mother, who warned I'd be sorry if my hand became imprisoned in a fruit jar. Secretly, I wondered about that. With a hand in a jar, I would not be an efficient aide.

After jars were washed, I was entrusted with the fruit preparation step. Applesauce was laborious. Apples had to be peeled, cored, quartered. Mother did not use a food mill. When the applesauce was cooked, she beat it with an egg beater. We didn't like chunky applesauce.

Mother did not trust me to fill and seal the jars, which were then covered with a floursack dish towel and cooled on the counter. Mother then counted off the "pings" as the lids announced they had sealed.

Our canning season, blessedly, was shorter than in some households. Tomatoes were the only vegetable Mother canned. She distrusted home-canned green beans, and since we had no fruit trees that produced, and few orchards were in our area, we canned whatever we could come by: apples, peaches, prunes, apricots, pears, tomatoes, watermelon rind pickles.

When cucumbers began coming on, she made pickles. Jams, jellies, apple butter had to be made. Chokecherries were gathered for syrup for pancakes.

Prunes and apricots were my favorites to can. They didn't require peeling, slicing or blanching, and mostly their seeds came out without a fight, whereas peaches required not only blanching but often held on tenaciously to pits.

Canning would have been more pleasant in the winter. It called for a roaring fire in the wood stove. That in itself was almost a full-time job. If one put in wood that was too big, the fire might not be hot enough. If one put in wood that was too small, it burned too quickly. Steam wafted up from the dishpan of fruit jars, the big kettle of applesauce blurped up its heat, the stove put out great waves of torridity, even the hot fruit jars on the counter radiated warmth, not appreciated on a hot eastern Oregon day. Although the kitchen door usually was open, when Mother filled the jars she closed the door because drafts might crack jars.

After the jars were checked to make sure they sealed, I took them down to the cellar. That was more fun than bringing up empty jars. Now, all grouped neatly together were the burgundy-purple prunes, the amber peaches and apricots, the tomatoes, the benign-looking jars of applesauce. And when canning was all done, Mother would come down to see the display and revel in her season's work.

Although I didn't enjoy canning season, I learned from it more than just the open-kettle canning technique. First, I discovered that applesauce was quite tasty as dessert on a wintery evening. And I learned that canning is planning for tomorrow, which is a wise thing to do. It's better yet to plan for winter and best of all to plan for a lifetime.

In canning, there is such a lesson. It may be unpleasant to go to the doctor or dentist today, but when one does, it helps to guarantee one's health tomorrow, next winter, next year. And, although it's more fun to spend money today than plan for tomorrow, it's good to remember that winter comes.

My Mother and my grandmother would be aghast if they knew that I did not can nowadays. I have no cellar with shelves of home-canned food but the lessons learned from canning apply to many things. Plan ahead for winter. Plan ahead for tomorrow.

CHAPTER 52

A Turn on the Dance Floor

Cowboy boots stomped out the rhythm of violin, piano and drum. Dust from spangles on the dance floor in the community hall was thick as smog on a Los Angeles freeway. Monument was having a Saturday night dance. Dances back then were about the only entertainment for Monument and other Grant county towns. And come summer, with start of haying and harvesting, those dances, like winter clothes, were put away until fall.

We had no movies, library, museum, lodge or service clubs. Dances were our major social outlet, and they were rip-roaring endurance contests. They started about 9 p.m., after ranchers finished chores and donned their finery: white shirts with long sleeves rolled to midarm, cowboy boots — and cowboy hats usually worn on the dance floor.

People flocked to our dances from Long Creek, Dayville, Spray, Kimberly. From Monument, we might drive 120 miles round trip for dances in Canyon City or Hardman.

These dances were no 9-to-12 affairs. At midnight, instead of "Good Night, Ladies," we stopped for "Supper." At that break, everyone lined up at the rear of the hall, where long tables draped in white butcher paper offered paper plates, $1 each, for sandwich, pickle, Jell-O fruit salad and cake. As per social structure, eating was not the big thing. The big thing was if and whom you went to supper with. If a girl came with a date, he was expected to take her to supper. If gals didn't come with a date, the evening's success hinged on being asked.

Almost as important as having a supper partner was having a partner for every dance. To sit on the bench was akin to being a sub never sent in the game. Our hall had two big wood stoves at opposite ends of the room, with single, available girls clustered at one end around the stove, not so much to keep warm as to provide visibility to the guys who stood around the stove at the other end of the room.

As musicians launched into a number, male dancers listened long enough only to determine if it was slow or fast — one they could dance to — and then swooped across the hall to get to the eligible gals first.

Since dances were our important social event, it behooved every young person to know how to dance. We gals had an advantage over guys. During noon hour at school, we danced with each other. Some girls led as ably as men, and we girls often danced together at the public dances showing off the steps we'd mastered. But if the guys sometimes lacked Fred Astaire footwork, they compensated with robustness and enthusiasm. Mostly they were big strapping kids, and their partners hoped mightily they wouldn't end up with a foot crushed by a cowboy boot.

Monument's dances had no lovey-dovey cheek-to-cheek dancers who covered only three feet or so during an entire dance. Fast dances were our favorite, but neither musicians nor dancers could survive a fast number every time. We eastern Oregonians covered ground when we danced, and "She'll Be Comin' Round the Mountain" brought out our best. Round and round the hall we'd go at full tilt, racking up half a mile in a single dance.

I've never known the name of one dance that we particularly enjoyed and that was popular then. With arm about partner, we jutted out the other arm — hands joined with partner, and pointed straight ahead. Instead of facing each other, we looked ahead and then, like a military march, headed purposefully across the dance floor. After going a goodly distance in one direction, suddenly at the whim of one's partner, the direction was reversed and we headed in the opposite direction.

But it was the square dances, interspersed occasionally with the round dances, that brought out the athletes. Here, the stalwart ranch kids were at their best. When the caller shouted, "Swing your partners," the ranch boys did so with vim. They lifted partners off the floor — even sizable partners

— and swung them around. We partners hoped the guys wouldn't get dizzy. And mostly, we hoped our partners wouldn't fall down, not uncommon during a square dance.

At the start of our dances, spangles were distributed generously on the floor to make it slippery. If the spangle dispenser was overly generous, the dance floor could become as hazardous as black ice on an Oregon highway.

For girls, these public dances were lessons in learning how to follow. Even coming with a date, you probably danced with him only the first dance, the Supper dance, and "Home, Sweet Home." The rest of the evening, you hopefully danced with a different partner each dance.

That taught a girl how to dance. After having Joe as a partner, who did a tricky chicken-scratch step, it then took concentration to follow your next partner, Bert, who never heard the music but pushed his partner around the floor in a fast waltz, regardless.

Our dances had no closing hour. If, at 2 a.m., musicians showed signs of wearing down, the hat was passed as inducement for them to play on. At times when I went to dances a long way from Monument I got home as Mother was cooking breakfast. She'd ask if I had a good time, who was there, and if there'd been a big crowd. And then after we'd talked a while, with aching feet and hair the color of dance hall dust, I'd go to bed — happy that I'd had a supper partner and danced almost every dance.

As I dropped off to sleep, I was looking forward to the next dance. I loved those dances as long as a cowboy boot didn't crush my foot.

CHAPTER 53

The Circus Caused a Stir

Only once while I lived in Monument did the circus come to town.

For the hundred or so people in our town, that was a momentous happening during those Depression years. Even the old-timers could not remember such an event ever before.

But one aspect of the circus I particularly remember. It was when Mother said, "No."

Long before the date of the circus, word of its coming got around. Advance people came, put up posters and arranged for a site and other aspects of their visit that was probably the most important happening in Monument since high water and ice took out the bridge across the John Day River.

It surely was not a big circus, but it was of size enough to awe us. We were not mobile people. Almost anything from the "outside world" impressed us. The day before the circus was to start, trucks with animals, cages and all the baggage that goes with a circus, trundled into town. And as soon as the first truck arrived, party telephone lines started ringing. Everyone who wasn't otherwise occupied headed to town to see the circus go up — even kids from up Hamilton and Courtrock way.

My brother, Jack, and I hiked to town as soon as we heard. There in the square of little Monument, circus workers rushed here and there, unloaded trucks, took care of animals, assembled props for the tent. Forming a fringe all around, we locals gathered to watch.

Pretty soon, a circus worker came over to us onlookers and said that if there were any boys in the crowd who weren't afraid of work, they could earn tickets to the circus by watering animals and helping put up the tent.

Up went the hands of just about every boy — including that of my little brother. And before long I saw Jack carrying a bucket of water to the animals and grinning as if he'd just won a new saddle.

We high school girls —not interested in watering animals or helping put up tents — clustered around, giggling and watching and peeking at the animals. Whether there were tigers, lions, elephants, monkeys, I do not recall. That was not what I most vividly remembered about the circus coming to Monument.

A sizable crew — mostly young guys — traveled with the circus and before long, several started coming over and talking to us girls. They asked our names and if we lived in Monument and if we could ride a horse and rope cattle.

The workers — robust physical guys — were not at all averse to leaving their work to talk to us girls and one in particular spent much time with us.

Whether he was an uncouth fellow or smooth as a movie actor I cannot remember. But some of us residents of Monument were guilty of being awed by anyone who came from more than 50 miles away. I am unable, too, to recall his name, if ever I knew it. But the rest of the incident I remember well.

As the afternoon waned and we girls were about to head for home, our new circus friend took me aside — and asked me for a date.

I was astonished: A circus worker who had traveled all over the country, perhaps had a date in every town, was asking a homespun Monument girl to go out.

Momentarily I was speechless — stuttering and nonplused — then just as I was about to say yes, I thought of Mother and that she would undoubtedly throw up her hands in despair and think that all her training had been for naught if I accepted a date with a perfect stranger.

Finally I blurted out — and it sounded so childish and juvenile — that I would first have to get permission. I'd have to ask Mother. I thought at that point he'd laugh and walk away, but he said, "OK," when I said I'd let him know later.

Hiking home, I was as excited as if I'd been named Miss Grant County. I could scarcely wait to tell Mother and get permission.

Mother was getting supper when I got home. My brother was still in town setting up tents and watering animals. I told her about all the commotion in town and then I got to the exciting part.

"Mother," I said, "you won't believe this, but one of the guys at the circus asked me for a date tonight. That'll be all right, won't it?"

My Mother, making sourdough biscuits, stopped what she was doing — hands floury and doughy — and turned toward me. I'd never seen her look so aghast.

"Elaine," she said, and her voice was higher than usual, "I never thought a daughter of mine would even consider such a thing. You certainly are not going to have a date with a circus roustabout that you've never seen before — and will never see again."

"Mother," I said defensively, "it's not as if he's a guy in one of the circus sideshows. He's not the fat man or the thin man or one of those rubber-faced people who can make a thousand faces. He's one of the workers."

"That has nothing to do with it," said Mother. "The answer is no."

I was reluctant to give in. "I'm not exactly a child," I exclaimed, trying to think of other arguments to advance my cause.

"Elaine," she said, "We are not discussing this further," and back to her biscuit-making she went.

Disconsolately, that evening when we went to town I looked up my newfound friend. I felt like a 10-year-old when I told him sorrowfully that I could not go because Mother had said no.

Now, years later, I still often think of that incident. And one day when it again came to mind, I chanced to think about dates I'd had with different guys albeit never with a circus roustabout. I had lots of dates with Homer who became my husband — and before that I'd gone out with ranch guys and college kids and a sailor and the postmaster at Canyon City. And then one day, in mature years, as I recalled that circus-date incident, realization came.

Despite my posturing and arguing with Mother — and my apparent disappointment with her answer — I am quite sure, after due reflection, that I was much relieved when she said no.

CHAPTER 54

Tales of the Mountain Ghost

In eastern Oregon we grew up with stories about cougars, or mountain ghosts, as they are sometimes called.

We didn't often see those ghosts, but legends about them were told and retold.

Cougars were the only wild animal in that part of the country that we thought might likely harm us humans. Bears frequented the high mountains and might be unfriendly if one picked huckleberries in their patch when they had a cub nearby. But those bears weren't of the grizzly variety and we never heard of one claiming a human victim. And bears were more forthright than the big, stealthy cats.

One legend told in Monument was about the Lesley girls walking home from town one night. Sometimes, when I walked home in the dark from a school event, the cougar legend came to mind, but never did I have proof of stalkers as did the Lesley girls.

Sarah and Judy Lesley lived about two miles from town, and, one night as they walked home, they had the feeling they were being followed. Walking home after dark was not unusual for them, but this uneasiness about being followed was. It was an eerie, unexplainable feeling. They stopped to listen but heard nothing. Still, the girls had that strong sense that something was behind them — and not far behind. They became more and more uneasy and were relieved when they reached home without mishap.

Next morning, they told their family about the experience. Knowing that the girls were not alarmists, an older brother went back toward town to see if he could see tracks as evidence of their stalker. There in the dusty dirt road, he found the girls' footprints, and intermingled with them, the tracks of a huge cat, a mountain ghost.

My mother was certain she once encountered a cougar in our chicken house. Late one night, she heard a terrible commotion among the chickens. It was not unusual for coyotes, raccoons and skunks to partake of our chickens or eggs. Not wanting to awaken my stepfather, Mother started for the chicken house. Next morning, wide-eyed, she told her mountain-ghost story. She was certain that, the night before, she had frightened away a cougar.

Although cougar stories were told in the Monument area, sightings were infrequent. Nor do I remember that ranchers in the area lost livestock to cougars, although coyotes relished not only our chickens but also turkeys and sheep. One way to distinguish a cougar kill, we were told, was that if a cougar did not eat all of its kill, it covered the rest with brush and returned for a later meal.

Those mountain lions were no pussycats. They weighed about 160 pounds, were about 6 to 8 feet long and Paul-Bunyan strong. They could drag about five times their own weight, leap about 20 feet in one bound and jump from a 60-foot tree or cliff to their quarry below.

In an old encyclopedia, I read: "Cougars do not attack man." But, what with increased sightings of these cougars, pumas, or mountain lions as they are called, and the proliferating humans crowding them from their habitat, that no longer is true.

Another aspect of the cougar mystique is its cry. Old-timers in Monument who had heard it, described it as being similar to the keening cry of a baby, enough like a human child to make one's hair stand on end in the dark of the night. We were told that one immediately recognized that sound despite never having heard it before.

As these panthers lose their habitat and seek a new home, they are more frequently seen. Seen, or unseen, the stealthy mountain ghosts provide material aplenty for legendary tales, especially around a campfire on a dark night.

CHAPTER 55

Dreams of Driving Cattle

If I'd been a boy, the summer job I would have died for was trailing cattle from Monument to Heppner.

Cattle buyers in that era did not come to Monument with big trucks to buy and haul away cattle. Many cattle ranchers depended on Chance Wilson to trail their cattle to market.

Chance was Cattle Drive King around Monument. He lived up the mountain road at Top in a ranch house painted tidy white. There weren't many white ranch houses around Monument.

When we first moved there, Chance was a widower. His first wife, Ona, died in 1920. He was a little man, lean and sinewy, with barely enough flesh to hold his body together. Underneath the cowboy hat that he always took off for ladies, his eyes were squinty, so that one could scarcely see their twinkle and latent little-kid impishness. Always he wore cowboy boots, which made him look a bit taller. His jeans were faded and discolored from saddle wear.

When he came to our house, instead of sitting on a chair, he liked to hunker down on his hips, with handrolled cigarette at the ready, as friendly and gregarious as his cattle dogs.

Each summer, by horseback, Chance drove cattle the some 60 miles to Heppner. Round trip took about seven days. And, although his cattle dogs were of inestimable help, Chance hired a couple of lucky high school boys to also go on the drive. He never hired girls — and Monument offered scant opportunity for high school girls to work during the summer.

It was by happenstance that I became a sort of participant in those drives. Chance married Millie Jackson, a widowed schoolteacher who lived in Monument and taught the first four grades. Millie's youngest daughter, Mary, and my older sister were good friends. After Chance married Millie, she went by car on the cattle drives. Each day, she'd go ahead to where they spent the night, set up camp and have a meal ready when the horseback riders (and cattle) arrived.

When Millie made those trips, she'd first come down to see my Mother and ask if my sister — and I — could come stay with Mary while she was gone,

That was a wonderful week. As a younger tag-along, I was humble as could be to be included. When Millie arrived home and drove into the yard in advance of the riders, always she brought presents. One year, she brought each of us material for a dress, and we were delighted. Perhaps my Mother was not. Neither my sister nor I would make those dresses and that then meant added tasks for Mother during the summer, when canning, gardening, cooking and cleaning claimed almost every moment.

In truth, I knew few actual details about the cattle drives and, years later, when I tried to find someone who had gone on those drives, it was too late.

But in mind's eye, I picture it all: Swinging into the saddle early of a morning in Monument with bedroll tied on the back of the saddle and heading the herd out across country toward Heppner. Out across Sunflower Flat, where for miles and miles sunflowers grew to the exclusion of about everything else, their dried leaves sounding almost like firecrackers in late summer as the cattle plodded through them. Then through ponderosa pine country where the pine trees were so tall, the sun scarcely penetrated and fallen needles so carpeted the ground that it was sound-deadened, and soft and spongy for the tired cattle to walk on.

I wondered if there were corrals along the way where the cattle were kept at night, or whether if I had been on the drive, I might have been detailed to keep guard all night.

I never knew whether Chance, on his route to market, followed the dirt road that wound through the unsettled country between Monument and

Heppner or whether he blazed a trail. In either case, it would have been necessary for him to scout the route before the drive, making sure there were springs or creeks to provide water for the cattle, horses and men.

How large the herds were, I never knew. Nor did I know whether it was necessary for him to arrange for hay or other feed en route, or whether there was sufficient grass for cattle to graze. That would have been of considerable concern to the ranchers, whose cattle he was taking to market. Those ranchers wanted top weight for their cattle when they reached market. Pounds meant dollars — dollars that were, perhaps, their only cash crop for the year.

I wondered, too, if on one of those drives, the cattle had ever been spooked by a sudden noise, causing them to stampede.

And then I imagined, finally as Heppner came into view, the sense of achievement from the drive — and the excitement of again seeing civilization after days on the trail: people, houses, a courthouse, bank, stores, even a hospital in the town that suffered that terrible tragedy in 1903 when a sudden flood destroyed much of the community.

I was, of course, never hired for that exciting cattle drive, and today no cattle are trailed from Monument to Heppner. But perhaps had I been offered the job, as badly as I wanted the job and a chance to earn some money, I might have learned that it was not as I had dreamed it would be. Perhaps after a week in the saddle from daylight until dark, going without shower or bath, sleeping on a bedroll on hard ground, chasing all day those recalcitrant cattle that wanted to take their own route, and so saddle sore after seven days of riding that I could scarcely stand — or sit — then perhaps, I would have admitted that it was not my dream job after all.

CHAPTER 56

Mother Was Glad When They Left

Once a year — like Christmas and Thanksgiving — the custom threshers came to our ranch, but threshing was a happening that Mother dreaded. If ever a rancher's wife put her cooking reputation on the line it was during this annual event.

We didn't have freezers, so food could not be prepared in advance.

Making the pies, cakes and yeast rolls, shelling peas and peeling potatoes all had to be squeezed into the hours between breakfast and dinner, and again between dinner and supper. Breakfast preparation started sometime between evening cleanup and dawn.

Long before daylight, oil lamps burned in the ranch house. Hot biscuits were in the black tin pans, kept warm on the open oven door. Potatoes were frying along with bacon and venison steaks. The gravy, stirred up in cast-iron fry pans, followed. Pots of coffee were on the back of the stove. Eggs would be fried just before the men sat down.

The custom threshing crew traveled all about the country, sleeping in barns or haystacks at the ranches where they came to thresh.

They put in long days — but no longer than the rancher's wife. Luckily, the threshing operation at our ranch usually took only about a day. But a woman could be unlucky and have them for more than her share of meals.

If the threshing machine were moved a considerable distance from one ranch to another, it might leave right after dinner and be at the following ranch for supper, necessitating preparation of two huge meals — supper and breakfast — before the machine threshed a single sack of grain. Then, if the next ranch was distant, they would stay another meal in order to have half a day to move. There was no waiting until the threshers came to your door. Their schedule was tight. That meal had to be ready. Those ranchers who had a sweeping view of the road or highway that approached their spread were lucky. They could see the thresher long before it arrived at their ranch, a great hulk of a machine moving slowly, clumsily down the road, and visible far in the distance.

The food had to be ready when the crew came to the house. By the time workers washed up in the grey washbasin, the vast assortment of food was dished up and on the table.

This was the opportunity for the woman of the house to display her specialties: the apple preserves made by one rancher's wife; the cabbage cooked by another of Dutch ancestry; the angel food cakes by another. Each tried to outdo all other ranch wives.

Threshing crew members reveled in all that good food.

"I never tasted anything like it," one crew member recalled. "All of the food was wonderful."

"When I got home I nearly starved to death on the regular meals my wife was fixing," said another crew member who traveled with a threshing crew for 70 days one season.

The coming of the thresher to a ranch was a little like the coming of the clan. There was much conviviality, as if it were a social occasion. And in a sense it was.

No longer do ranch wives have to dread the coming of the threshing crew and the cooking that went with it. Nowadays, if a rancher does not have his own machine, a custom thresher travels to the field before hay is cut or stacked. The thresher operator travels alone. He takes his lunch, and returns home at night.

The new machine is a precision piece that gleams in the sun and often has air conditioning. It works efficiently and methodically and spurns the help of laborers and sociability.

But somehow it will never replace those threshing banquets and the convivial threshing crews dressing in the dark, perhaps huddled before a straw fire on a frosty morning.

Sometimes progress makes one wonder and sometimes it makes one sad. But my Mother would have been delighted not to see the coming of the threshing crew each year.

CHAPTER 57

Our Dear Feathered Friend

Our eastern Oregon ranch animals, except for horses and dogs, did not become part of our family.

They were "working animals" and worked for their keep. The chickens laid eggs. The cows gave milk. The sheep and steers provided us with cash crop. But then along came Terethbert the turkey. He was a different kind.

During the Depression, Mother, in an effort to bolster our cash flow, raised turkeys — no great number, just a few dozen. She sold them when they reached market age, with a few saved out for our holiday table at Christmas and Thanksgiving. The turkey raising was no great success and lasted only about one year with several gobblers remaining in residence as holdovers. They were eaten as the holidays rolled around — all except for Terethbert — a lengthy name for this unusual bird so mostly we called him "Turkey."

In truth, he deserved a name like Terethbert. We had never had a turkey with personality before, but this gobbler oozed individuality.

He roamed the ranch at will, perched in the barn with the horses at night, although the barn was a considerable distance from the house and we worried that he might be a catch for the coyotes. He did not associate with the chickens, regarding them as of inferior social status. Mostly, he spent his days around the house, rating himself as more closely related to humans than any other living thing on the ranch.

We began noticing Turkey's depth of character one summer when, after dinner dishes were washed, Mother, my sisters and I retired to the porch. Inevitably, Turkey, being of a social nature, came to join us.

By then, he had reached full and sizable maturity with magnificent plumage of which he was extremely proud.

Whether to impress us, or deeming that we needed entertainment, or perhaps because he had no mate of his own species and thinking we might suffice, he began putting on his daily show for us as we sat on the porch.

There in the yard, he strutted back and forth before us, stretching out splendidly the wing on the side facing us, so fully extended that the tips of the wing feathers dusted the ground. For eight or 10 feet, he strutted, and then turned around and came back, this time showing off his handsome wing plumage on the other side.

One didn't pat a turkey or reward him with treats, but our gobbler seemed not to expect such.

He took satisfaction from his performance, confident that it was appreciated and aware that we gave him full attention.

As he grew older, perhaps lonely with no turkey friends and refusing association with the chickens, he spent more and more time around the house. When we left the house, he followed us about like a dog. When we went on hikes, Turkey came along, too.

We often walked up on a little knoll behind the ranch house which provided a commanding view of the Blue Mountains and the meandering John Day River. Terethbert began going, too, following us all the way to the top, a good mile or so. Having then enjoyed the panorama, we ran pell-mell down the steep incline. Turkey did not run well downhill, but to keep up with us, he scrambled along madly for a few steps and then, with wings outspread like a condor, managed to become airborne for some six or eight feet. A strange procession we made coming down that hill.

As Terethbert became a steady companion, and as Thanksgiving approached, with him our only remaining bird, we began to have misgivings. How does one enjoy a drumstick from a turkey that goes on walks with the family and offers entertainment on lazy summer afternoons?

Although customarily on the ranch we acknowledged that animals were raised for sale or slaughter, thereby stifling excessive emotional reaction,

Turkey presented a different situation. Yet what was Thanksgiving without turkey? And Terethbert was our only source. Boyer's Cash Store at Monument offered no holiday birds.

On the calendar that hung on our kitchen wall, November came up. I did not ask Mother how she would resolve the dilemma. I knew my stepfather, Lynn, would be the designated killer of Terethbert and it was true that he had not been as attached to the bird as we who had been around the house. But it was not just the act of killing but of bringing him to our Thanksgiving table.

As the time drew near for making pie crusts and cranberry sauce, our phone rang and our neighbors, the Owings, asked our family to come for Thanksgiving. Not only were we delighted to do so, but this was reprieve for Terethbert. Terethbert seemed to know, too. He strutted a bit more proudly, gobbled happily and stayed even closer to the house, except for his nighttime perch in the barn.

Then about mid-December, realization came again. Would Terethbert be our Christmas dinner? We could not expect another invitation to solve our problem. I overheard Mother say to Lynn that Terethbert would have to be our Christmas dinner,

I couldn't imagine celebrating Christmas by serving up Terethbert. But early one morning about a week before Christmas after Lynn went to the barn to feed the horses, he came back with sad news. The coyotes during the night got our Terethbert. His beautiful plumage was scattered all about the barn.

Mother was able to get a turkey from neighbors, but I ate little at Christmas dinner that year.

CHAPTER 58

None of Us Became President

Only four were in my high school graduation class at Monument and none of us became president.

We had a ready explanation for that. All four of us were girls, and women in that era were not considered seriously as presidential timber. Our entire student body consisted of about 25 kids and our staff was miniscule: one combination principal, teacher and boys' basketball coach — traditionally a male. And one combination teacher who taught shorthand, typing and other classes, directed three plays per year and was girls' basketball coach — traditionally a woman.

Long before graduation, which was early in May, a representative came to Monument and we graduating seniors chose our commencement announcement. Although we would be graduating in a few weeks, it now was time too, to choose a motto, as well as class colors and the flower that was to be "ours." Those momentous choices required as much deliberation by us seniors as writing the U.S. Constitution. The motto we selected, which was quite original and hopeful, was "Onward and Upward." Our colors, requiring careful choice since it would profoundly affect the rest of our days, were blue and gold. Kids in eastern Oregon didn't know much about flowers so that choice was simpler. We had no access to orchids or gardenias. We settled for a rose.

After much consideration we then chose the style of our graduation announcement — which we ordered in great quantities. Although the population of Monument was perhaps 125, with far fewer households than that, we expected to send an announcement to every household within a 25-mile range. If we knew their name they received a graduation announcement, and sending of that announcement was tantamount to receiving a gift. The year we four girls graduated, the popular gift was underpanties. I received 17 pairs — including a set of seven, each of which was embroidered with a day of the week.

Seniors at Monument did not wear caps and gowns. We girls wore formals. Since Monument had no stores — except for Boyer's Cash Grocery which did not carry graduation dresses — our dresses were ordered from Sears, Montgomery Ward or National Bellas Hess. Each catalog had perhaps half a dozen possibilities, so there was decided possibility all four of us might appear on commencement night in Wards' princess style, with sweetheart neckline and puffed sleeves at $14.95, plus postage — from page 38 in the catalog.

Because my older sister then worked in Portland, I prevailed upon her to shop for me. I felt quite puffed up to have a dress that did not come from a catalog. She chose a pink floor length, with flared skirt and little covered buttons that marched from neckline to hem.

Commencement services were held in the auditorium of our high school building — at night — since ranchers worked outside from dawn until dark at this time of year. We seniors, not exactly overflowing the stage, sat on folding chairs in our regality — along with the chairman of the school board who solemnly dispensed our diplomas, handing one to each of us without regard to name, so that after commencement we had to seek out the one that was our own.

Guest speaker often was the Grant County School Superintendent whom we viewed with considerable awe since she came from John Day — the metropolis of our county. This designated speaker spoke eloquently, steering us down a path that led to a role that we would eagerly assume, if not as president — although that was a distinct possibility — then at least as dedicated and worthwhile citizens.

We graduating seniors performed too: valedictorian, salutatorian, we willed everything to under-classmates, and we prophesied.

We also had music. Usually Mrs. Canova, our teacher, who accompanied our singing, chose "The World Is Waiting for the Sunrise," for us to render.

The auditorium was heavy with the fragrance of whatever flowers happened to be blooming that spring and that could be gleaned for decorations. Lilacs were a favorite — and historically we knew that Aunt Tee, the widow lady, had huge lilac bushes in her backyard whose blooms she would sacrifice for commencement. Iris multiplied nicely in eastern Oregon. Our town had a few snowball bushes and peonies sometimes were in bloom. We piled the flowers in big buckets and festooned them across the front of the stage.

Everyone came to our commencement exercises — not just the families of our graduates. After all, everyone was invited. And everyone from in and around Monument continued the celebration afterwards at the public dance — until 2 or 3 a.m.

Looking back, none of us seniors was surprised that our class didn't provide a president. But there is much to be said in our behalf. We four learned self-sufficiency. We did not become a burden to our state. None of us was ever arrested for a horrible crime — requiring support by taxpayers as we lolled in jail. None of us sold dope, robbed a bank, or blew up a Grange Hall.

Not only in Monument but all across the country, few classes provided a president. But most class members became good parents, hardworking job holders, people who mowed their lawn, solicited for the cancer drive, took library books back on time — and even served as Room Mothers.

CHAPTER 59

Legs Were Meant for Walking

In eastern Oregon, one didn't walk to school in patent leather Mary Janes.

Serviceable black lace-up shoes took us kids to school.

That trail from ranch to town — about a mile and a half — followed the dirt road that meandered off through mahogany and sagebrush, veered off on a dusty path, and followed the Kimberly-Monument county road to cross another field, where we crawled through a barbed wire fence to arrive at school.

My appearance when I arrived was of little concern to me. It was sufficient to know my hair was combed earlier that morning. Only if the needle grass in my anklets poked me uncomfortably did I think to remove them. My shoes had never been introduced to polish. Crawling through the barbed wire often was unfriendly to clothes. I did not arrive at school as a cute little girl, but not for the world would I have missed those walks to school.

I was by no means the only one who came to school on foot. We had no choice. The one school bus in our district served kids only from the Kimberly area. Parents did not then drive kids to the school door. Some ranchers did not have cars, and no Monument High School student had his own car. Some high school boys, who lived in the community called Top, rode horseback. One girl, Coramae, who lived at Top, walked those five miles to school morning and afternoon for four years.

But never did any of us feel abused or put upon. That walk provided lessons as valuable as some learned at school.

For one thing, we learned what legs are for. Nowadays, when kids are driven half a dozen blocks to school, one wonders if that's a lesson they'll learn.

And that hike to school was also a "sanity walk." If I huffed off to school in the morning, thinking my mother had unreasonably disciplined me, the "sanity walk" helped me to understand that her actions might be because she was bone tired from caring for four children, a garden, chickens, cooking and cleaning.

Trudging along on a level with the sagebrush, it's easier to figure things out than when you're riding to school in a car. You're spending a lot of time with yourself.

When I failed to get a coveted role in the school play and did not believe I could survive that disappointment, by the time I walked home, I realized I'd already survived for a half hour and that the next half hour would be immeasurably less miserable.

From that walk, we came to have a first-hand acquaintance with the flora, fauna and the weather and its moods: sullen before a thunderstorm, prancy on a spring day, lethargic in the sultry autumn, harsh when it dropped below zero.

And every day, the flora changed its clothes for us, except for the stolid sagebrush that did little to meet the seasons except for its pungent bloom. One day, there was snow on the ground. Another day, the dark ground appeared with the melting. One day, little green spokes of emerging wheat and rye poked up in the fields. One day the chokecherries blossomed. One day, I took home to my mother a bouquet of white syringa for the kitchen table.

Our trail crossed a little unnamed creek that went dry in summer. In the spring I always stopped to check the varying water life: water skimmers, little black bugs that scooted around like jet skis, little creatures that carried their houses around with them.

And there was the wildlife. Jackrabbits bounced away through the sagebrush like kangaroos. If we chanced upon a rattlesnake, we always tried to kill it if there were rocks nearby. Without rocks it was no easy matter. More often than rattlers, we saw the big harmless blow snakes that closely resembled rattlesnakes, except for head and pointed tail. The blue racer snakes lived up to their name and raced away before one could ponder whether they were poisonous.

The wary coyotes, we saw infrequently, and the deer kept mostly to higher ground. In the spring when the ticks came out, we found them, sometimes attached to our bodies, looking like little gray, blown-up balloons. We lit wooden matches, blew them out and held the hot match against the tick, whereupon it backed out. Otherwise, if one tried to pull off an "attached" tick, the head sometimes remained imbedded. Only occasionally did a resident come down with Rocky Mountain spotted fever.

A small part of the route to town was along the county road. Mother constantly cautioned me never to accept rides from strangers. But I knew of no little kids who had been carried away or accosted by strangers in those days, and I readily accepted rides, not advising my mother of such. The people who offered me rides I found interesting. They queried me about where I lived and how old I was and where I went to school, and I queried them. Today, under no circumstances would I accept rides from strangers, but I learned then that there are ever so many nice strangers.

Not long ago, when I chanced to expound on the good of walking to school, our son said to his dad, "Now we're going to hear about when Mom hiked five miles to school through the snow and the sleet and the hail."

I laughed and offered no rebuttal, knowing that only those who have walked to school can appreciate the lessons learned therefrom.

CHAPTER 60

Under the Oregon Sun

Even before the sun crept over the mountains to the east of Monument, it forewarned of another sweltering day. Heat had declared war on eastern Oregon.

For eight days, temperatures had topped the 100-degree mark. Now on another airless morning, the sun inched over the horizon, seeking out first the tops of the junipers, then advancing higher, its already hot rays finding the sage and rabbitbrush. Then the ranch house felt its early morning attack.

Inside, we were up before dawn — going outside to scan the skies even before the fire was laid in the cookstove.

"It'll be another scorcher," said Mother from the porch.

The sky was cloudless. The sun already was on the battlefield. It would be unforgiving again today.

In a sense, the heat helped the rancher. The hay was down in the field.

No rancher wanted rain at this point — about the only time when rain was not welcome. Rain could mean extra work — even ruined crops. The mowed and raked hay already was shocked, and rain could mean that every shock would have to be turned so the hay could dry. A heavy rain might ruin the hay.

So the ranchers battled the heat as best they could — up early to be out in the fields for as long as possible in the cool of the day. If a breeze came up it was an ally. If the humidity was unusually high and the air as still as in a closed-up car, the sun then won that day's battle. The dust in the hayfield stifled breathing and was gritty in the mouth.

This was not the era of sophisticated farm machinery with air-conditioned cabs. Horses did the work — telltale sweat foaming on their flanks and shoulders and beneath their harness. Hay hands pitched hay onto the wagon and another worker in the wagon drove the team from shock to shock, and distributed hay evenly in the rack. When the wagon was so heaped with hay the men could scarcely crawl atop, they headed for the stack where the cattle would be fed come winter. Once unloaded, back to the field they headed for another load.

"How many loads?" Mother always asked when they came in for dinner. The more loads today, the fewer to be done on the morrow.

Hay hands wore big straw hats, sometimes cowboy hats, long-sleeved chambray shirts and Levis, seasons removed from their original stiff blue. They drank water often from the gallon jug — shared by all — that previously held vinegar. This glass jug, now wrapped in burlap, was soaked with water before going to the fields. That helped keep the drinking water cool.

In the ranch house, the wood-burning cookstove — the only means of cooking the food — also radiated heat despite open windows and doors. After the meal, the fire often was stoked to heat dishwater. In late afternoon, the winds might bring relief, although at times it was a searing, punishing wind that pulled remaining moisture from the soil and wizened humans as well.

Although our kerosene refrigerator was an ally, it was not efficient enough to freeze ice cubes. But with luck, even in summer one might still have ice in the ice house.

On summer evenings when daylight hung on as if there were no tomorrow, it was a relief when the sun finally crept behind towering West Gulch that overlooked our ranch. Late in the evening, we sat on the back porch and without forks, ate slabs of watermelon from our garden, spitting the seeds into the yard.

The turtledoves told us goodnight — soft, wistful "hoo's" — and the summer nightlife came out: bullbats that swooped alarmingly close in search of flying insects, moths that came seeking light from our kerosene lamp, huge black beetles that took to the air and when they crashed on the porch, sounded like a .22 shot.

As with us humans, the livestock could do little to combat the heat. The saddle horses early in the day made their procession from pasture to watering-trough at the ranch house, where they squabbled as to which would drink first. Dozing then, in the shade of a juniper, one leg akimbo, they were glad they were not working horses that day.

The cattle grazed early in the day so they, too, could then seek the shade. The chickens, their combs limp as an oft-washed shirt, ceased scratching for food. The dogs dug holes in the yard, much to Mother's displeasure, and sent out notice that they were not to be disturbed with working orders.

Part of the war against the heat meant providing water for stock and animals. If saddle horses were being kept up in the barn, they had to be taken to water morning and evening. Water for the calves at the barn had to be supplied. Although the cattle that were pastured upriver on the Elder place had a spring as water supply, at this time of year someone every week or so had to make the six-mile horseback ride there to make sure the spring was not dry.

And the John Day River, where we kids cooled off on summer days, became sluggish and torpid, so that our mothers forbade us to swim in it for fear it had become contaminated.

Then one Tuesday morning, after nine days of hundred-degree-plus heat, the sun relented. Clouds rolled over Johnny Cake. From off across the mountains toward Hamilton, thunder rolled in the distance. A breeze sprang up — life-giving, cool. And the chickens began scratching. The cattle started grazing. The dogs decided to chase jackrabbits. The ranchers finished haying. Ranchers' wives announced, "It's going to be a lot cooler today."

Eastern Oregon ranchers not only had to battle hard times during the Depression, often they had to battle nature — and sometimes they won.

CHAPTER 61

Riding the Can-Opener of the World

Roads — whether rutted dirt roads, graveled county roads, or six-lane free-ways — open up the world. They take us to strange and beautiful places, places of opportunity.

Roads are like can-openers. They open a whole new can of contents.

From our ranch house in eastern Oregon, nestled at the base of a rim-rocked hill, we looked down at a long stretch of the Monument-Kimberly county road.

That road, too, was a "can-opener." From Kimberly, it led to Spray, Fossil, Condon — and thence to Portland, where there were escalators and movies and 5- and 10-cent stores, none of which we had in Monument.

Once a year we made that trip to Portland, where Mother's parents lived. I dreamed about that trip all year.

The day before we left, Mother fixed a huge lunch to eat on the way, including always fried chicken and a cake. Early in the morning, we started. One year, when we had a car with a rumble seat, my sister and I rode all the way to Portland in those open-air seats that provided fine views of wonders along the way. After the sagebrush, juniper and rimrock landscape came Condon's undulating wheat fields, then Arlington and the great Columbia River with barges working its waters, and trains and highways on both sides.

The Columbia made our John Day River seem like a little puddle.

Sometimes, at Celilo Falls, we stopped to see the Indians fish for salmon from precarious little platforms that extended out over the river. On the way home, we often stopped and bought a salmon from them.

Across the Columbia was the Stonehenge and mystic Maryhill Castle, where I was sure kings and queens lived. At convoluted Rowena Loops, I fervently hoped I would not get carsick. Always we stopped at Vista House, where we could see farther up and down the Gorge than we could see from the top of Monument Mountain.

Then Portland. To me, a 10-year-old, it was the biggest city in the world. The can-opener road had led us here to the ultimate.

Meanwhile back at Monument, since we went to Portland only once a year, the can-opener operated on a considerably lesser scale. The dirt road that led to our ranch house from the Kimberly-Monument county road represented scant "can-opener" opportunities.

From our ranch house, we could see the turn-off where our dirt road left the highway and snaked along through sagebrush for a mile or so before reaching the house. Any car that turned off the highway onto our dirt road was of immediate interest.

"Car coming, car coming," I called out if I were the first to see it. We had no steady stream of visitors arriving by automobile — most arrived by horseback or team and wagon. The visitor arriving by car might be a cattle buyer coming to look at the cattle. Or my mother's worry was that it might be the game warden coming to see if we had venison out of season. But I, at that age, when common sense was not as highly developed as imagination, dreamed that it might be a "prince," a date who decided that this was a fine day to come, unannounced, and drive me away to a movie in John Day.

During high school, there were days when I looked down at the cars on Kimberly-Monument road and wished with all my heart that the can-opener would open up roads for me. I imagined where the cars were going, imagined that I was in one of them, going away to school, to a job, to a career — new people, new places and everything that might mean.

Possibilities for graduated high school girls in Monument were mostly non-existent. Most of the girls got married as soon as they graduated. Monument offered no jobs for girls. Parents, during that Depression, could not afford to send offspring to college. Nor had anyone from Monument gone to college — except for acquiring teaching certificates — for as long as I could remember. I wondered what I would do after finishing high school, while I waited for someone to decide to marry me.

My shorthand teacher, Mrs. Canova, was my savior. Her home was not in Monument and she knew many people in John Day and Canyon City, the county seat, and she "snared" for me a job with the county agent in Canyon City.

I rented a one-room apartment in Canyon City — and I saved my money, the first paychecks ever received. I had a scholarship to Albany College (now Lewis & Clark College in Portland) at Albany, Oregon. I contacted the College and found an Albany family where I could work for room and board. And so one winter day, the can-opener went to work. It opened up a road. I was leaving Grant County to enroll at Albany College winter term.

Suitcase in hand, I left Monument. I cried when I said goodbye to my family and the dogs and the horses and the ranch that I loved so much, and I thought what a dunderhead I was to leave all this that meant so much to me.

And then the can-opener road down there, leading from Kimberly on beyond, sent out a reminder: What a dunderhead one would be, it reminded, not to partake of the contents of a newly opened can -- and the road that led beyond.

CHAPTER 62

Huckleberrying — What a Vacation

All year long, during the Depression, ranch families in eastern Oregon, looked forward to huckleberry season.

Cattle, sheep and wheat prices were so low there scarcely was a "cash crop" but that didn't stop those Grant County travelers. After haying they took their annual vacation. They went huckleberrying.

They didn't go by car — but by team and wagon. A whole caravan of them — perhaps 15 or more, with a wagon for each family, and an anticipated stay of some 20 days,

Jolting over backwood roads wasn't the most comfortable in the world, but mattresses and heavy quilts provided padding. Men drove the teams, and most wives rode up in front beside them. The kids piled in back or walked beside the wagons.

It was no small job packing for those vacations. Everything from tin washbasin to axe for chopping wood, to flour and baking powder for camp bread had to be brought along. No stores would be nearby if a ranch wife forgot something, although one of the other families on this vacation caravan would probably provide it.

The huckleberries, after being picked were canned in camp each day.

So fruit jars, jar lids, sugar had to be taken along — along with the milk pan in which the berries were cooked.

Picking those berries was no easy task. It took concentrated effort to pick two gallons a day. In Monument, Mattie Stubblefield was a renowned

185

huckleberry picker but she had been at it a long time. She started picking as a little girl while living in Fox Valley. She and her two younger sisters rode horseback to pick the berries. Back they'd come in the evening, lard pails filled and tied in flour sacks to the saddle. There was no money for fruit jars so the berries were dried — spread on a clean cloth and left in the sun.

Usually caravans from Monument headed for the Galena and Granite areas for their huckleberrying. If berries weren't good there, they headed for Dixie Mountain near Prairie City. To get to Granite took at least two days. The vacationers camped along the way with wagons at night arranged in a circle, as when wagons headed to Oregon Country when crossing the plains. Meals weren't potluck. Each family cooked its own over a campfire.

Once they found good berries, camp was pitched. Fir boughs were cut for softer sleeping on the ground, but there was no lying abed on this vacation. Come daylight, campfires were built, breakfasts cooked, lunches made. Then "vacationers" rode horses or mules until they reached a good picking area. Men, women and children picked — men usually better pickers than women. Rivalry was great between families to see who could pick the most. One Monument resident, in particular, "Oat" Stubblefield, was known to resort to friendly trickery in the patch. Pickers in a spot lush with berries would hear Oat's "Halloo". "Come see the berries over here," he'd call out. "You won't believe how big they are."

Whereupon, pickers always eager to find a patch even better, hurried over to his "great picking area" only to find Oat grinning — and a patch not nearly as good as that which they'd left.

One of the fastest pickers in the Monument area was Cliff Merrill who once picked an astounding five gallons in one day.

Picking ended about 3 o'clock every afternoon in order to get back to camp to can berries by open kettle over the campfire.

Then came suppertime: perhaps mulligan with chopped cabbage, onions, carrots; fried potatoes and onions; beans, or stew. For dessert, just syrup, or biscuits and syrup — or huckleberries. Lacking refrigerated food chests and fresh milk, canned milk was a necessary staple. Some liked that canned milk better than fresh cream on their berries.

And almost always there was "camp bread," made in some families by the men. In the Stubblefield family, Murd was more adept at it than Mattie. Bacon grease was first melted in a big black frying pan. Baking powder dough was patted to fit the pan, like a giant pancake, and cooked on one side until sizzling and golden brown. Then real skill came into play: the bread was flipped in midair, presumably ending up in the center of the skillet for cooking on the other side.

After supper, everyone gathered round the campfire to tell stories. But even though it was vacation, picking was the big thing. They would be up early the next day — and pick every day. Fruit jars couldn't be taken home empty. At vacation's end, the filled jars, wrapped carefully in newspapers, were loaded in the wagon and the long trip started for home. Everyone had worked hard — but working hard in those days was taken for granted.

Huckleberrying had been a change of scene. And there would be huckleberries all winter long — wonderful huckleberry pies and dumplings.

Said Mattie, when asked if she didn't tire of the purplish fruit after picking for 20 days, her emphatic answer was, "Oh, my no."

Those huckleberry vacations were memorable. And one has a feeling that those who experienced them, might do little complaining about today's scant leg room on airlines and the pretzel fare.

CHAPTER 63

New Teacher in Town

About the last of August they came, driving up the graveled road, from Kimberly to our little town: the incoming new teachers at Monument High. Our high school had only two teachers and some years, both were new. Mostly they stayed few years in Monument.

The coming of the teacher was an important event and we lost no time in assessing the new arrival. If Millie Strong met the new principal in the post office, she was likely to be on the party line with her critique as soon as she got home. Our 125 residents didn't have a local newspaper, but party-line handled news pretty aptly.

"I just don't know about him," said Millie to Linnie Fields. "He seems likeable enough but he looks so young."

Whether the school board in those days interviewed a teacher in person before the hiring or whether it was a mail-order thing, I do not know, but Monument may have been near the bottom when a teacher was applying for a contract.

Monument had little to offer excited young teachers who wanted to imbue kids with a thirst for knowledge. For one thing, our school had only about 24 high schoolers and not all were thirsty. The boys, especially, were mostly interested in just putting in their four years so they could start ranching.

Then, too, housing was a problem. We had no condos overlooking the John Day River, no apartments, no motel — although Mattie rented rooms in her two-story white house. And Mattie was a good reporter. After Mr. Deidricksen moved into one of her rooms, it wasn't long before Monument's population knew that he had two suits hanging in his closet — worn on alternate days.

If a teacher was married, it took much finagling to find a house to rent.

Nor could an unmarried teacher expect to find available singles in Monument. Girls, as soon as they graduated from high school, usually married the fellow they'd been going steady with for maybe a couple of years. By the end of four years, just about everyone in high school had paired off with everyone else. It was quite surprising that in such a small group they found that "one person in the world."

If there was an eligible single, Monument had its eye on that teacher and the single gal to see if anything developed.

Nor would a new teacher discover much in social life at his new home. Our town had no movies, except for a traveling show that came irregularly, and it was 60 miles to John Day, our big town.

Monument had no fine restaurants — usually no restaurant at all. Boyer's Cash Grocery was the only store. We had no library, concerts or civic clubs, although a little group of Legionnaires occasionally met.

We had dances — big dances — attended by all. When I was in high school, principals were always male and if they were unmarried, rather than dance with the young married women, they danced with us high school girls, although it is not much fun to discuss algebra on the dance floor.

But those teachers probably worried little about filling spare time.

They coached the basketball teams — boys and girls — and track. They directed the plays. They taught half of all classes in high school. They staged commencement exercises, wangling perhaps to have Estelle Boyer, the county school superintendent, come as speaker. One nice teacher, Mrs. Canova, helped start a little band and our group sometimes was hired to play at dances.

Mostly, the two grade school teachers were married locals who remembered having your dad in their class. A long-time married woman teacher, who lived on a ranch near us, rode horseback some five miles to school, except in the winter, when she boarded in town. The school board must have been mightily relieved to look to locals year after year. Nobody much questioned whether they were good teachers. They were a constant in our schools — a constant Monument was lucky to have.

Yet teaching in Monument, compared to teaching in pioneer Oregon 100 years earlier would have been a joy. Teachers back then might live with one family for a month, then another. In some schools, length of time a teacher boarded with a family depended on the number of kids — the more kids a family had in school, the longer the teacher boarded at that home. They probably shared a room with one, or many children.

The school house in those days was usually a one-room log building, cracks filled with mud and sticks, puncheon floor, and, lacking desks, homemade benches. Salary was perhaps $25 a month. Because of inclement weather and lack of transportation, schools often were held only in the summer, and come winter, the teacher had to look for another job.

Compared to all that, Monument was a winner, and I can't recall that any teacher at Monument was ever a dud. They came, knuckled down and gave it their best. And their best was usually memorable, so much so that, in retrospect, it's the teachers I remember and not the significance of the square of the hypotenuse.

Especially, I remember what a high school principal, Henry Kauppi, wrote in my autograph album. He wrote: "Rivers run, stars shine, worlds turn — and so must you keep seeking knowledge and bettering yourself for evermore."

It's too bad that we kids didn't appreciate those teachers more. But then, that's probably still the case in a lot of classrooms today.

CHAPTER 64

The Night When Outhouses Fell

In the unincorporated community of Monument the prescribed Halloween trickery in the 1930s pertained to outhouses. There were about as many outhouses in town as there were people.

Pushing over outhouses on Halloween was as traditional as turkey on Thanksgiving.

We weren't juvenile delinquents when we did that, we thought it was expected of us, and there wasn't much else to do.

This activity didn't lend itself to preschoolers and grade-school kids. It was the high schoolers who made Monument's Halloweens memorable.

We needed some big kids for Halloween and many of the 25 or so high school students were big strapping ranchers' sons who seemed too old and too physically developed to be in high school.

The first outhouses we chose belonged to the people we didn't like. If, when we were loud and noisy in the post office as we waited for the mail, Mr. Onergan commented about our behavior or scowled at us, he was sure to be visited on Halloween night.

If there was someone for whom we had a pronounced vendetta, our goal was to tip over the outhouse while the owner was in it.

Although details as to how this tradition evolved are hazy, I remember the Halloween when some became bored with the annual routine. We yearned for a more memorable trick — something that would stand out in Monument Halloweens.

Someone devised the idea of using the horses that many kids rode to school, to pull Mr. Onergan's outhouse across town.

Mr. Onergan would have to search for it the next morning. And since he didn't own a horse, would have a difficult time getting it back.

We had no law and order in Monument. State Police from John Day headquarters were our gendarmes. But one Monument resident took pride in his town and disliked our Halloween shenanigans. He had himself deputized and set out to make Monument more of a model town.

That annoyed the high school boys and one Halloween night a confrontation occurred.

The details of what happened that night, in the dark with horses, outhouses, high school kids and the deputy, were never clear. The deputy may have been given a horseback ride. Someone may have shoved someone and that person shoved someone in return. But all Monument was abuzz when charges were filed against the big boys.

The trial took place in nearby Long Creek — and the entire high school student body attended. The boys were exonerated.

People in Monument still talk about what happened that Halloween night. But kids in Monument still, for many years — until those outhouses went out of vogue — continued to celebrate All Saints' Eve that way.

CHAPTER 65

We Need Activists, Too

No one likes animals better than I and I'm glad that we have activists who stand up for their rights. But some animals are downright cruel to us humans. It would be nice to have someone represent us people against animals, sometimes.

Two of our saddle horses on the ranch, Skinner and Ginny, continually out-thought and abused us humans. We didn't keep them in the barn but let them out in the pasture unless we rode every day. If I decided to ride over to see my girl friend, I'd have to go out in the pasture and bring them in. Skinner and Ginny had things their way in the pasture, communing with the other horses, eating grass and, once a day, coming in to the watering trough at the barn.

Those horses sensed when I planned to ride them. Unfailingly, on those days, they didn't come in for water until late in the day, so I had to go after them.

Our pasture wasn't the Willamette Valley kind: a little green handkerchief of land outlined by fence. Our horse pasture, about a half-section of land, had hills, canyons, knolls, rimrocks, junipers, sagebrush — great places for animals to hide. Our horses, tucked away in a canyon, couldn't be seen until you walked to the edge of the ravine and peered in. Sometimes that meant walking about as far to get the horses as it was to town. When I showed up out there in the pasture, Ginny and Skinner didn't have to be masterminded animals to know what came next. One of them was going to furnish transportation for me, with a tight cinch and a weighty saddle.

Their remedy was to not get caught. Our hoped-for procedure to catch a horse was to take along a halter, put a rope around the horse's neck, put on the halter, leap on the horse and ride bareback to the house. That wasn't what Ginny and Skinner had in mind.

Every time I'd get within 10 feet of them, they'd trot away — just out of reach. I had one trick that was supposed to work. I'd hold the halter behind me so they couldn't see it. I suspected that Ginny and Skinner thought that was as humorous as could be.

After we'd chased them all over the pasture and tried to catch them 10 or 12 times, we began to feel considerably abused, but no people's rights advocate ever interceded on our behalf.

We needed such an advocate for our sheep dog named George — one smart canine —when on a hot day he was sent to bring back stray sheep. He went willingly as far as the nearest sagebrush where he would lie down, unseen, in the shade.

We also needed an advocate to stand up for our rights with Billy, our big buck sheep with menacing curved horns. My stepfather Lynn was not intimidated by Billy, but Mother was afraid of him and was careful never to be alone around him. One day, she and Lynn were walking to the barn, and Mother was a few steps ahead of Lynn. Old Billy sneaked up from the rear, went around Lynn, charged Mother and knocked her down.

And if you've tried persuading a bunch of yearling calves to go into a corral when they didn't want to, you know how abusive animals can be to humans. All family members, including my 9-year-old brother, were called into service for this task. With corral gate open and family strategically stationed, Lynn attempted to drive them into the corral. Despite all efforts, they'd break away and we'd start the round-up all over.

People, after all, took up the plight of the spotted owl and the plover. It hardly seems fair that animals can "abuse" us humans and no one steps forward to intercede in our behalf.

CHAPTER 66

Dark Not a Fearful Thing

You couldn't be afraid of the dark if you lived in eastern Oregon. If you grew up there, you became a pretty good friend of the dark. Before the Rural Electrification Act came to little towns like Monument, ranch houses for the most part lacked electric lights. Ranchers had no yard light that protectively beamed light on surrounding areas, and no lights at the barn or corral.

Coal oil lamps or Aladdin lamps provided light for homes. Coal oil lanterns provided light for the rancher who fed or milked after dark. Often a rancher's night vision was so keen — especially on moonlit nights — he didn't bother with lantern.

When I was growing up, I did not know about the "kids being afraid of the dark" syndrome. Perhaps that was because of daily lessons received. When we went into a dark room, no flick of a light switch immediately dispelled the darkness. If you were to be in that dark room only a couple of minutes you didn't light a coal oil lamp. Nor could you pick up the lighted lamp in the kitchen and carry it into the dark room with you. Family members in the kitchen wouldn't appreciate being left in the dark.

In addition to dark rooms, lessons in becoming acquainted with the dark included being sent to the cellar. It took much doing for me to pass that lesson. The cellar was scary. It was not so much that dark that I feared — of and by itself — but what the darkness might conceal: scorpions, black widow spiders, snakes, strange animals that might decide that cavern, with its dirt walls and floor, was a fine home. When Mother sent me down in the cellar to get an onion, in the darkness I was certain when I reached in the bin, I would touch some furry wriggly object, or something slimy and cold.

We also got to know the dark because of our outdoor plumbing. At night no little tiki torches illuminated our way to our outhouse, about a block from the house. I did not usually mind that trip at night. There was no reason to mind it — unless the weather was bitterly cold. And then, although I never let Mother know, sometimes in the night I did not go all the way to the outhouse.

I thought it quite funny, during hunting season one year, when a Portland man and his wife came to stay with us and go deer hunting with Lynn. That woman had never learned that the dark could be companionable. When she had to go to the outhouse after dark, she insisted her husband go with her.

Mother, who did not grow up in eastern Oregon, quickly learned that inhabitants there couldn't be afraid of the dark. In part, that was because of her chickens. She regarded her flock proprietarily — they were hers — and she considered them a valuable asset. Their eggs were essential for breakfast every morning, and for baking. They also provided her with fried chicken, roast chicken, chicken and dumplings, chicken and noodles.

She was ready to go to bat for her chickens anytime. So, if in the night she heard a fearful squawking and cackling from the chicken house and suspected that a skunk, an owl, a coyote — or even a cougar — might be killing her chickens, she rushed to their defense.

She could not wait to awaken Lynn, who did not regard the chickens with the same passion as did Mother. It might have taken considerable time to impress upon him the urgency of the situation, so Mother, the instant she heard the commotion, leaped from bed in nightgown, taking time only to put on shoes, and rushed to save her chickens. Never having gone with Mother to the chicken house for such "confrontation," I do not know her method of defense when she got there. Did she go to the chicken house door and shout "Shoo?" Did she pick up a piece of wood to throw into the middle of that melee? Did she use that wood to hit that intruder over its head? Regardless of her type of attack, I thought how courageous of her to enter that dark chicken house — not knowing what might await.

There was another way we kids had to become comfortable in the dark. When I was in high school, there were numerous school activities at night: such as basketball practice and play practice for the three programs the high school presented each school year.

We kids were expected to get that mile-and-a-half back to Monument by our own power. Parents didn't hop in the car and run us back to town and then come back to pick us up when we were ready to come home. Many parents didn't have a car. Their transportation was by horses, so we kids walked back to town at night in the dark — and after basketball practice, or whatever, walked home. There were no ranches between our ranch and town, no light of any kind.

I could have carried a lantern — regarded as being somewhat "sissy" — but I walked in the dark. Some of that distance was along the highway, some through open fields, some through dense growth of sagebrush and mahogany.

The trail to town — where it left our dirt road because it cut off distance — was well worn. I was not afraid of getting lost. I knew the trail well enough to have almost walked it with eyes shut.

And never when I walked that route in the dark, do I recall of having been frightened by an unknown sound, or rustling in the sagebrush.

Nor, looking back, was there reason to have been afraid — and the dark became a friend.

That's not to say that I regard the night with the same liking as day, but there are times when the darkness is to be dearly loved: on the Fourth of July at the Jaycee fireworks when their magnificent display is silhouetted against the velvety black sky. Or, in later years, sleeping in sleeping bag in the back of the pickup in eastern Oregon and looking up at the Milky Way and its myriad of stars; or on a black night on the Amazon when in a little dugout canoe we found fireflies that thought we Americans needed light and cut the darkness so that we almost could read by that illumination.

Darkness in those Depression years at least meant that we had no electrical bill to pay. But it's harder to get to know the dark nowadays. Nor am I offering eastern Oregon lessons these days in how not to be afraid of the dark.

CHAPTER 67

Chores Don't Stop One from Dreaming

I recently met a woman — not young — with amazing drive and energy. She attributed her work ethic to growing up on a dairy farm.

She said, "I tell my daughter all the time to be sure to give her kids chores to do, but my daughter says there just aren't any jobs for her kids because they live in town."

I never lived on a dairy farm, but we had cows, and one of my chores was to bring in the cows every evening.

It wasn't a job that really honed one for the vicissitudes of life. It didn't demand judgment or skill. But I didn't find that job at all unpleasant. I'd head off down the little trail that wound through the sagebrush, and although I made that trip every day, there always was something different to see.

Sometimes a baby rabbit darted across the trail and sometimes I'd discover a crude turtledove nest barely encircling the ground around the eggs. In the spring there might be ragged ladies to pick: fluted, ruffled, pink flowers I've never seen grow elsewhere.

Our cows didn't try to make my job harder by going off to some little draw where they were out of sight until one stumbled onto them. They were led by their stomachs to where they found the best grass. Back they went to that site, day after day, until the feed was exhausted and the stomach led elsewhere. And once I found them, they were not devilish about being persuaded to come home.

Chores with regard to the cows were just starting when they got into the corral. They had to be milked and fed, the calves had to be cared for, and after the milking came the separating task.

Separating the milk was another of my chores. It didn't exactly teach a marketable skill, and it took not one bit of judgment or discernment. Although it was my job for several years, you could, on your first attempt, have done it as skillfully as I.

First one poured the still-warm milk through a flour sack cinched with clothespins atop the separator's big bowl, making sure spigots were turned off. Now a sizable bucket was positioned under the milk spigot, and a smaller lard bucket was placed for the cream.

As one turned the handle at a moderate rate, results were immediate. Bluish fluid poured from milk spigot; from the other, golden cream in a stream about one-fourth the size of the milk flow.

That was all separating required: just turning the handle around and around. But what it taught was patience, that not everything required of us in life is going to be earth-shaking, that if you're doing something uninspiring, why not dream of something that is inspirational while you're doing it, such as going away to college when you haven't the least idea of how it is to be funded.

After the big bowl atop the separator was empty, water was poured in to flush out the separator parts. Next morning, after the morning milk was separated, the separator was taken apart and washed. One important lesson I learned was to never wash a separator in soapy water. It made the separator parts slick and unpleasantly slimy.

When I washed the separator, I had great admiration for the inventor of that machine. Its numerous parts included a myriad little cups, all fitted into one another. It took a bit of practice to put the separator back together. I never figured out how all those little cups and the rest of the machine worked, but I didn't have to know. Turning the handle was enough.

Families not living on a farm don't have the variety of chores to assign kids to teach them that in grown-up life, the same old jobs often have to be done day after day. But there's more than one way to turn a separator handle.

Such chores teach that while turning the handle, it's possible to dream of other things.

CHAPTER 68

Haystacks Denoted Happiness

In late summer, when fields and hills in eastern Oregon took on the tawny coloring of a lion, the most beautiful sight for a cattle rancher was his haystacks.

Neither stock market's rise and fall, nor price of gold determined what kind of year was in store for those cattle ranchers during Depression years.

Size and number of haystacks and how long cattle would have to be fed during winter were determining factors.

For much of the year, our Hereford cattle fended on their own in Grant County. They foraged grass and palatable things that grew on the lower rims of Johnny Cake, the banks of the John Day and the slopes of Wall Creek.

But as grass petered out in the fall and threat of snowflakes was in the air, ranchers started riding for cattle to bring them nearer ranch houses where there were haystacks and cattle would be fed during the winter. Old-timers said that a cattle rancher had it made — even in the Depression — if he had sufficient cultivable land to raise hay to care for his cattle's needs. He could then probably make mortgage payments and preclude foreclosure.

But Nature was sly and cagey and a rancher never knew how his crops would turn out.

Not just the rancher, but the rancher's entire family was involved in this tussle. The rancher's wife worried along with her husband. And the kids — even those not old enough to understand — sensed the worry if all was not well.

If spring was late and weather unduly cold, seeds might not germinate, or young seedlings might rot.

If spring rain did not materialize, sometimes the wheat and rye would not sprout.

Even if grain sprouted, if there was not enough moisture, it shriveled and died.

Although little could be done in such an event, ranchers hovered over sick crops as a mother hovers over a sick child. After supper in the spring, my stepfather Lynn and Mother often walked down to one of the fields to see if grain was yet sprouting.

If the ground was dry to the touch, each day they watched anxiously for signs of rain. When Nature was friendly, the rains finally came and fields turned green, Lynn smiled more often and Mother hummed when she stirred up the pancakes for breakfast.

How long cattle would have to be fed during the winter varied considerably — since that, too, depended on the weather.

Seasoned ranchers benefited from their experience. Lynn knew about how many bundles he'd feed per head per day in those days before haying became highly mechanized and our cranky old binder string-tied the hay into little sheaves. Past years were a good indication as to when feeding would probably start. Likewise, a rancher had a good idea as to how long he would have to feed before cattle could be turned out in the spring.

But there were the variables. Often in very cold weather, Lynn fed more hay per head than if the weather were temperate.

A good rancher didn't try to fool his cows by cutting back on what he customarily fed if stacks grew alarmingly small. Experienced ranchers knew that was false economy. When ranchers sold cattle, come summer or fall, price was based on size and condition of cattle. In the long run, it was better to use the last scant cash for hay.

As winter progressed, Mother and Lynn watched anxiously as the stacks went down. It was especially worrisome if crops that year had been sparse and Lynn had banked on an open winter and an early end to feeding. In the fall when crops had not been good, deciding whether to buy hay was a little like a game of roulette.

If a rancher bet that he wouldn't need additional hay and then had to buy more, he'd lost the game. The later in the winter a rancher bought hay, the higher the price. Some years when it seemed feeding would never end, hay became scarce. When it could not be bought locally and had to be hauled — perhaps from Prineville or Redmond — cost was even greater.

Our ranch had no permanent pasture and cattle fended for themselves after winter feeding when grass took the place of hay.

Often in the spring when we were still feeding, Mother and Lynn after supper walked to the grazing areas, hoping to see sprouting new grass that could support the cattle.

During good years, when crops were lush and tall and rye and wheat heads pregnantly plump, there would be no doubt that the hay would last the winter.

Those years when Nature and the good earth were kind, Lynn came in from the fields, during haying, jovial and smiling, and we kids knew that all was right in our world. The rye field down by the river was yielding half again as much as last year, he said, and the wheat crop over by the mountain road was as heavy as he'd ever seen. And Mother would just about get choked up and we kids could feel the happiness as if it had been passed along the table like a plate of biscuits.

Late in summer when haying was over and the hay in stacks, and the fields and hills had again taken on that tawny gold, Mother and Lynn often walked down to the fields below the house. And there they would stand for a moment looking at their haystacks — enough feed to last the winter — the most beautiful sight in the world.

CHAPTER 69

City Folk in the Country

When we lived in eastern Oregon and occasionally visited my grandparents in Portland, I suspect that we were thought of as rubes who gawked at tall buildings.

But we got even. When Portlanders came to eastern Oregon, we often whispered to one another, "Aha, another tenderfoot."

It wasn't as if we were looking for someone to belittle as a tenderfoot. Rather it was a kind of retribution because we sometimes felt awkward and gawky when we went to "The Valley." When we got on a streetcar, we didn't know the amount of the fare or where we were supposed to put the money. We were almost hesitant about stepping onto an escalator, and we didn't trust self-operated elevators.

One criterion for determining whether an eastern Oregon visitor was a tenderfoot was how he got on a horse. If he used the saddle strings, the saddle horn and even the horse's mane in an effort to rappel himself onto the horse's back, he received the tenderfoot rating.

But if, when mounting the horse, he held the saddle stirrup in one hand and with agility put the proper foot in that stirrup and easily swung himself into the saddle — all the while holding the reins so his horse wouldn't bolt — we immediately accepted him as a brother.

After our Willamette Valley visitor managed to get on the horse — if the horse was patient enough for him to do so — we quickly saw whether that person was a tenderfoot by the way he sat in the saddle and rode. If he jiggled and bounced around in the saddle, especially when the horse trotted, he accumulated tenderfoot points. If he held onto the saddle horn with one hand, he accumulated more and if, when the horse galloped, he held desperately to the saddle horn with two hands, hopefully trying to hold the reins at the same time, he automatically received full tenderfoot rank.

Another sure sign of a tenderfoot was if he could not assemble a cream separator. This, of course, is a simple operation after one has done it a few times, but for the visitor who perhaps has never turned a separator, putting all those parts in order was comparable to assembling a computer today. We might also classify a visitor as a tenderfoot if he was asked to gather eggs at the chicken house and, while there, encountered a hen, who feeling the pangs of motherhood, was reluctant to leave the nest and the eggs accumulated under her. Hens then became brave creatures — even when affronted by a huge human. Their beady eyes stare at the oncoming attacker and the beak goes into action if one comes near. A tenderfoot doesn't get the eggs and lets the hen win the round.

We knew, too, when we had a tenderfoot on our hands by the clothes that he wore. If his jeans were so new they crackled when he walked and so stiff that he could scarcely sit in the saddle, he lost 50 points in our ratings.

He lost more points if he wore a new plaid cotton shirt with metal snap buttons, pristine and unfaded from even an hour in eastern Oregon sun, a cowboy hat so new we expected to see a Minnie Pearl price tag hanging from it or cowboy boots as shiny as a little girl's patent leather Mary Janes and so uncomfortable he could hardly hobble out to get on the horse.

One way to make certain you would not be classed a tenderfoot was if you could harness a horse — especially since a good many of us who lived in eastern Oregon could not do so. It helped, too, if you could saddle your own horse and throw that saddle on the back of your steed without the stirrup hitting you in the face.

Our animals could tell a tenderfoot, too. Especially animals that were bullies took advantage of them. A horse immediately knew if his rider was a tenderfoot and stopped to eat every choice bit of greenery along the way and poked along, head down, half asleep. But the instant an experienced rider got in the saddle, the horse held his head high and marched along like a thoroughbred, perky as could be.

The bulls and buck sheep, and even our mule that chased people, could all smell a tenderfoot and took after them with delight.

We gauged a tenderfoot by little things, too, such as lighting a kerosene lamp — not that it took skill or knowledge. But when you're doing something for the first time, it's more of a challenge.

We worried, too, if tenderfeet came in the fall to go hunting with Lynn. We hoped they knew how to handle a gun and weren't the kind who began banging away when they heard something move in the brush without knowing what they were shooting at.

Almost as important as being able to safely handle a gun was to not get lost when they were hunting. When Lynn directed them to go around the knob at the end of the wheat field, cross the little canyon and head up the draw until they came to a bunch of quaking aspens, where they'd meet after making their drive for deer, they often wouldn't find that patch of quaking aspens. Then all of us locals worried that we had a lost hunter on our hands.

There was another way we knew a tenderfoot. If they visited in the spring, when ticks were nearly as plentiful as the flies in the summer, they had to have a lesson in "tick-ology." If perchance, a tick latched onto a visitor, burrowed its head under the skin and gorged itself with blood until it was about the size and color of a blueberry, our visitors became downright distraught and wanted to jerk that offender off its skin. We locals knew, of course, that trying to pull it off could leave the head imbedded, and that putting a hot match against the body of the tick made the tick back out in a hurry.

We definitely knew we had a tenderfoot on our hands if he couldn't shut our gates and so left them open — and that we could not forgive. And some of the residents from west of the mountains were so inordinately afraid of rattlesnakes they never came to visit.

So it was that we got even when we feared we acted like rubes on one of our few trips to Portland. We merely waited for visitors to come visit us, and then we smiled at each other and said, "Aha, a tenderfoot."

CHAPTER 70

At Age 16 I Didn't Know

We had scant money when I was growing up. But even had we been wealthy I suspect that would not have changed many of the things that I did when I was 16.

Such as lying all day in my bathing suit in the sun on the banks of the John Day River. I wish I had then known that that exposure might have repercussions some day. We eastern Oregonians thought the sun was kind to the skin. Lack of money was not to blame.

I wish I'd known at 16 that there was something called dental floss, and that I had used it religiously from that time hence. But as I recall, dental floss was then something not found even in the homes of the wealthy.

I wish I'd known at 16 how ridiculous it was to smoke cigarettes so peers would think one worldly and sophisticated — likewise trying to inhale, and strangling in an attempt to prove that sophistication. But a generous allowance wouldn't have helped and perhaps made cigarettes more available.

I wish I'd known when I was a high school senior that the lead role I didn't get in the school play was not going to destruct my life. I wish that instead of staying home from school the next day so I wouldn't have to face the gal who did snare that role, I'd known that I would have felt better had I sought her out to congratulate her. But I can't blame poverty for this.

Nor would money have helped me to have been more concerned about my appearance. I wish I'd known at 16 years that my "back" was as evident as my front when it came to appearance. No parental suggestions ever persuaded me that uncombed hair on the back of my head was seen by everyone except me. Likewise shoe heels worn off to the nub until they canted, crooked hosiery seams (until the blessed day when they did away with those) and slips that dangled a bit in the rear.

I couldn't accept that these were evident to everyone but me. Only if I could have turned my back around to become my front would I have admitted these grooming errors,

I wish at 16 there had been classes that had taught me how to be a better wife and mother and that these would have been the classes I never skipped and in which I got A's. But lack of money was not to blame.

I wish at 16 I had known the freedom today's kids know when it comes to school apparel. Never did I head for school those four years of high school in anything but a dress. No girl wore jeans, pants or shorts to school but I cannot fault poverty for that.

I wish I'd known when I was 16 that when a boy asked me to dance whom I secretly regarded as somewhat socially "beneath" me, I would have liked myself better had I not turned him down. Wealthy parents would not have made me a better person.

I wish at 16 I'd been able to talk more easily to people of different ages. I wish I'd made more effort to talk to little kids, and people old enough to have grey hair — even my parents. I was to blame — not lack of money.

I wish at 16 I'd known that it wasn't egotistical to like myself. I wish I'd known it was as important to like myself as it was to like all other mankind but poverty had nothing to do with how I regarded myself.

I wish at 16 I could have foreseen that the boy I had a crush on, albeit rumored to be a bit "fast," would grow up to be an addle-headed nincompoop.

I wish I had known at 16 that patience did not arrive with the suddenness of a Mt. St. Helen's eruption. Perhaps if patience had been seeded at 16, it might have developed full bloom.

I wish at 16 I had known what the college professor told us as college seniors: "An education is something to be lived with — not on."

I wish I'd known at 16 that tidiness was not something that could be learned as one learned fraction tables and that it had to be practiced. Tidiness, I discovered in later years comes not with the turn of calendars.

I wish I had known at 16 that parents do not live forever and that 16 was surely not too early to let them know how dear they were to me.

I wish I'd known at 16 how much one could enjoy the outdoors and animals and people and books and just living — although maybe it is more fun to become aware of that every year.

How nice it would have been had I known all these things at age 16. But ignorance — not poverty — was to blame.

CHAPTER 71

Little Dog, Big Lesson

Our little dog, Major, never dragged any of our family from a burning building or pulled away one of us kids as we were about to step on a rattle-snake. But to us Major was a hero.

We nicknamed our dog "Majey." He was a precocious, cocky, short-haired and short-eared, black-and-white spotted little dog of nondescript breed. It was unusual for us to have a dog like Majey on the ranch. Maybe one of us kids brought him home as a puppy, or he showed up as a stray at the ranch house and we didn't have the heart to send him on.

Mostly, we didn't keep dogs for entertainment. Our working dogs — Binky, Rusty and George — helped with the cattle or sheep. But although there really was no place for Majey on the ranch, he developed his own niche. He was a companion and a comrade.

For a time we thought about trying to make a cow dog of Majey. But he was so little, we feared the cows would regard him merely as an annoy-ance and perhaps hurt him, whereas the cattle had considerable respect for our bigger dogs.

Majey was not at all upset that he was the only thing on our ranch that did not work. He acted as if he were royalty, despite his unknown heritage. In cold weather when we let our dogs sleep inside, Majey crowded out the big dogs from the warm space behind the kitchen stove, and the cattle dogs did not know how to deal with that feisty little creature who acted as if he owned the ranch.

Although Majey had no assigned tasks, he seemed always to have important things to do. When Mother fed the chickens, Majey went along to run away the guinea hens when they pestered her flock. And often, Majey headed off into the sagebrush on his own, as if checking the ranch to make sure all was well. Sometimes he came down to meet me when I walked home from school. I wondered how he knew the time, but there he'd be, coming down the trail — my little white and black dog — stepping along as if he were marching in a parade, head held high as if he were the most important animal in the world.

Majey was really more my dog than anyone else's. The big dogs worked for Mother and my stepfather, Lynn, but I was not one of the managerial staff so I didn't often have jobs for them. When I went to bring in the cows or horses, the big dogs were not at all interested in going — perhaps because that smacked of work and they were tired — but Majey wanted to go. He accepted his job as escort for me as if born to the task.

As we headed down the trail, Majey had more stops than the mailman. Every sagebrush, every mahogany bush was checked for smells. Every tussock of bunch grass, rabbitbrush or needle-grass was an imperative stop. In between, he pranced along on his short little legs, looking quite out of place on a cow trail.

But one day, Majey headed off by himself, into the sagebrush to check on some important assignment known only to him — and he did not come back. We were terribly worried. That wasn't like Majey. He liked home life.

We wondered if a coyote had eaten him or if a rattlesnake bite had kept him from coming home. I hiked around the ranch looking for him, but there was no sign.

And then, days later, after we had given up all hope of his coming back, I looked out and there, creeping along the trail toward the house was Majey. He was crawling, scarcely moving, dragging his hindquarters.

We rushed out to him and, as I started to scoop him up to carry him, we saw his terrible plight. His hind leg was missing — clear up to the haunch where a raw, gaping bone extended with shreds of flesh and skin.

Lynn realized what had happened. A government trapper had set coyote traps in West Gulch and Majey, in his explorations, was caught in one of them. In order to escape, he had chewed through his own leg.

We wondered what to do. Monument had no veterinarian. There perhaps was none in Grant County at that time — nor could we have afforded one. Would it be kinder if Lynn shot Majey to end his agony? If he lived would he be able to get around?

At a family conference, we decided that if heroic little Majey had chewed off his own leg, he wanted very much to live — with or without that appendage. So we cleaned his wound, fed him all the best table scraps and treated him royally. Majey responded like the hero he was. He hobbled around a little here and there, and a gristly covering began to form over the wound.

And then one day when I was going after the cows, Majey, as if sensing where I was going, looked up at me pleadingly.

"No, Majey, not this time," I said, and patted him understandingly. "Maybe one of these —," I started to say, but Mother interrupted. "Why don't you let him go?" she said.

"If he gives out, you can carry him home. He wants to go. He wants to give this three-legged life a try."

And so I started down the trail slowly, slowly, with my dog following. For a time, he stumbled. His gait was uncertain and ungainly. But I did not want to turn around and watch because I feared it would embarrass him. We went a bit farther and I sneaked a glance back and I could have cried. My little Majey was prancing just a little bit. He was figuring out that three-legged arrangement pretty well. Despite a missing leg, he was going to get along just fine.

Majey lived many years after that. And he again became a cocky little dog who found it not at all a handicap to have only three legs. As agile as ever, he hurried around the ranch to take care of all his self-assigned tasks — without even finding it necessary to put that stub of a haunch on the ground.

Majey never saved any humans' lives, but our dog who chewed off his own leg was a real hero to our family.

He taught us two-legged humans how precious life could be and that even the most unbearable agony could be faced if need be.

CHAPTER 72

Christmas Is Candy

Christmas is Santa Claus, Christmas trees, manger scenes.

And Christmas is candy.

At our ranch in eastern Oregon when I was growing up, the ordering of the annual Christmas candy supply was an important event. Weeks before that wonderful day, Mother took out the Sears and Wards catalogs and we clustered around the kitchen table as she made out the order. Many times already I had studied the catalog pages where the candies were shown: peanut brittle, chocolate drops, gumdrops, orange slices, sugar crèmes, hard candy — and expensive chocolates that came in fancy boxes that we could not afford. Nuts, too, shelled or unshelled — one kind or assorted — were ordered from the catalog.

We had no choice but to get our candy by mail order. Our one general store in Monument carried no Christmas candy. Its inventory was candy bars. We lived almost 60 miles from John Day, our "big city" which had some 600 people. Although Christmas candy no doubt was available there, we did not often make trips to the "city."

So, there at the family table, following democratic procedure, we made our selection — about the same every year: orange slices, chocolate drops, sugar crèmes and peanut brittle. Occasionally we ordered hard candy, not because we liked it as well, but because it lasted longer than the more "gourmet" kind. If we ordered hard candy, we chose the kind that was "stuffed" and had chewy sweetness inside.

After the order was mailed, we waited impatiently for our big package to arrive at the post office in Monument. When a notice was put in our mail box advising "Please call for parcel at window," we knew it had come.

When we got home we opened the package excitedly to make certain that the proper candies had been sent. Plastic bags were then an unknown. Our candy came in unsealed paper sacks.

Although the candy came long before Christmas, it was put away until the big day. In order for it to be out of sight — and out of mind — Mother stored it in our attic.

For us kids it was never out of mind. Almost daily we lobbied Mother for just one piece as a pre-Christmas treat. Sometimes she agreed, and standing on a kitchen chair reached up in the attic to take from those paper bags the variety that each of us chose.

My choice was always a chocolate drop. I hoped it would have a lemon center because that was my favorite. I did not pop that candy into my mouth and eat it in one bite. With a toothpick, I made a small hole in the chocolate shell and bit by bit extricated the soft center. With care I could dig out all the center without breaking the chocolate, and then the best part of all could be savored.

Other than at Christmas we seldom had store-bought candy, but Mother often let us make fudge. It was a boiled mixture of sugar, chocolate and water. It was no gourmet concoction but for us it rivaled See's chocolates. We kids quarreled over who got to scrape the pan. Often the plate of candy was half gone before it was firm enough to cut.

In later years, after Homer and I were married, the scarcity of candy during the Depression seemed almost preferable to the over-availability of the candy supply.

As we shopped for Christmas we were constantly tempted by the huge boxes of chocolates placed in the center aisles. Those chocolates displayed on the lid of the box, were irresistible.

"We don't need all those calories," Homer would say.

"It's Christmas," I'd argue. "It's only once a year." Whereupon the five-pound box was taken home and put out of sight in the hall closet.

As with our candy that was stored in the attic, we remembered it much too often. After lunch, after dinner, before we went to bed, one of us suggested "just one piece of candy", whereupon we made our selection ever so carefully. If we erred and chose a chewy caramel instead of a gooey center, it was a disappointing choice.

In addition to the temptation of store-bought chocolate, candy canes and chocolate Santas, I felt compelled to make many batches of homemade candy.

It's hard to not eat a goodly portion as soon as they are off the stove. But there are alternatives to eating them all yourself. Hurry and take some to friends. Hide the rest, freeze several batches.

Then the doorbell rings and friends have brought you elegant offerings of divinity, creamy chocolate fudge, fondant, chocolate covered hazelnuts. As we guiltily think of calories, cholesterol, fat we consume, we rationalize that Christmas comes only a year,

And I think, nostalgically, that sitting around the table at our eastern Oregon ranch and ordering Christmas candy from the catalog will never come again.

CHAPTER 73

There's Never Been an Ugly Christmas Tree

Getting the Christmas tree was a ritual my older sister Lillian and I anxiously awaited in eastern Oregon.

We eagerly assumed the job that no one else wanted. My stepfather was far too busy with demands of a cattle ranch. Mother was inundated with household tasks of a family that included my younger brother and sister. Lillian and I categorized these two younger siblings as too little to go on that outing.

In November we started querying Mother as to when we might go. Our house was too small to accommodate a Christmas tree for two months so usually it was a week or two before Christmas when she agreed to let us make that important foray.

For our Christmas tree hunt we equipped ourselves with a saw or a little hatchet for chopping down the tree. Then as Mother bade us goodbye with the admonition, "Find a good one," we headed up the trail that led into the high mountain area we called West Gulch.

Said our little brother, disparagingly, as we headed up the trail, "Bring back a better one than you got last year."

Fir trees were not plentiful in that area of eastern Oregon. But in one canyon two or three miles away, Lillian and I long before had discovered the best source for Christmas trees. It was a hike we loved. That area seemed like a world different from the juniper-pine-sagebrush vegetation nearer our house. And in West Gulch there was an historic landmark which we always visited on our Christmas tree trek.

That landmark was the site of a long abandoned still, in the bottom of the canyon where a little stream had provided necessary water for its operation. There were many rumors about this illicit operation. We knew the name of the rancher who supposedly operated it. Although he no longer lived in the area, we knew some of his relatives.

This stop at the old still took considerable time. The workings of a still were totally unknown to us, but we imagined how the liquor must have been taken out by horseback, probably in fruit jars to eager customers who, because of prohibition, had difficulty in finding that product. After this stop we headed on up the canyon for the Christmas tree area. In this canyon, trees did not have benefit of much sunshine. And growing on the side of a canyon, they received that scant available sunshine on one side only. They also had to adapt to growing on an incline, so it was not easy to find a beautifully shaped tree.

Always as we left on our trek, we visualized the beautifully symmetrical tree we would bring home. But once at the site, as we wandered from tree to tree, we were brought back to reality. If the front of the tree was symmetrical and somewhat dense, the back had scarcely any branches at all. From a distance we would think we saw the perfect tree, but then as we inspected it closely, we discovered it had big gaping voids.

And there was the matter of size. Our little house could not accommodate a tree that would be impressive in a gymnasium. Yet we wanted as large a tree as Mother would condone. This, too, narrowed the field.

Then, just as we despaired of finding the perfect tree, we discovered it tucked away in a little draw, somehow overlooked on previous years. We inspected it from every angle, from above and below. True, there was a gap in the branches on one side but as Lillian pointed out, "That side could be turned to the wall." This was indeed our tree. It was beautiful. We hacked it down and triumphantly started home.

My Mother, sister and brother saw us coming and came out in the yard to meet us.

"Did you find a good one?" Mother called even before we reached the corrals adjacent the house.

"I hope you got a better one than last year," our young brother said.

"We really got a good one this year," I shouted from the gate.

"This is the best one ever," Lillian declared.

Proudly we bore it into the house not even letting them critique it before it was in the corner where we would mount this beautiful object. Lillian held it up so we could stand back and survey that handsome tree.

I noted — and hoped my Mother and brother did not — that there were gaps in the branches not noticed back at the site. And it surely was not as symmetrical as I had pictured it back there.

Mother, my brother and little sister stood back and looked at it. For a moment there was silence. "Oh, that's going to be a fine tree." Mother said.

"Where are the branches that are supposed to be on that side?" my little sister said.

"That's an ugly Christmas tree," said my brother.

Lillian and I were crestfallen. Perhaps we too now saw that our find was not the beauty we perceived it to be back in the woods. And how could we have a perfect Christmas if we had an ugly Christmas tree? It was Mother who rescued our Christmas.

She looked disapprovingly at my little brother, And then, "Oh, it's beautiful. There's never been an ugly Christmas tree!" she said.

CHAPTER 74

Wildflowers for Mother

On Memorial Day, I do not take flowers to my Mother's grave.

She is buried in Monument at the cemetery that is at the foot of a little bluff not far from the John Day River, where deer, in curiosity, often peer over the sagebrush during a service.

I, of course, was at her funeral but that was several years ago. I have not been to the Monument cemetery since.

For others, I go to cemeteries. I go each year, to the grave of my father, who is buried near Woodburn in a cemetery with a strange name: Belle Passi. I understand that it means "beautiful place," and long ago it was the site of a little Oregon town.

The marker on my father's grave is flat, as markers are required now to be in that cemetery. They are cold and impersonal. It calls to mind Flanders Field with its crosses row on row. At Belle Passi, the markers in those rows are as if manufactured in mass numbers, unlike the markers in the old pioneer cemeteries hereabout. Each of those old upright gravemarkers tells a story with eulogies, doves, lambs and ivy.

I take flowers each year to my sister's grave — and some years I manage to not cry — but I have not been to Mother's.

I do not know what kind of marker she has because I have not seen it. It will, no doubt, have her name and the date of her birthday — May 30, Decoration Day — and the date of her death.

It is not as if I am trying to deny my Mother's death. She has now been gone many years. Rather it is that I do not wish to think of her that way.

Instead, on Memorial Day, I think of her as a living Mother — as if it were Mother's Day.

She was a plucky, spunky lady, except that she was afraid to stay alone at night. If my stepfather were gone, my sister and I did not plan to stay the night with friends. Yet in the middle of the night, if she heard the chickens making a din — a sign that some varmint was trying for a meal — she got up from bed and headed for the chicken house, a good block from the house, to confront whatever it might be that was menacing her flock — be it skunk, raccoon or even cougar.

Often, she came down to meet me when I was walking home from school. Down the dirt road she'd come in her housedress. Women then were not yet wearing slacks and jeans and pants except to ride horseback.

Housedresses in those days were easy to find. Mother usually ordered hers from Sears or Wards. And often, in the summer, she wore tennis shoes — without socks. We did not often wear sandals around the ranch. They were little protection if one stepped on a rattler.

Her hair was black before she started turning gray, and it was induced to curl by a home permanent given to her by a friend, since we did not have beauty salons in Monument.

But even in housedress and tennies, I thought she was beautiful as she walked down the road to meet me. I thought her very much the gracious lady. When we once were shopping in Portland and were to meet at a designated place, we saw each other from half a block away and she smiled. Her smile, I always thought, put Mona Lisa to shame.

She was incredibly busy on the ranch: taking care of her chickens, picking raspberries, cooking, cleaning, washing, ironing, canning, mothering. But busy though she was, she wanted to be pretty, too.

If I wanted to especially please her, I gave her facials, although I knew not what constituted a facial because I had never had one. Mine were a poor substitute for those from a salon, but they pleased her: cold packs, hot packs, astringents, creams.

She hated it when her hair started getting gray and often inveigled me into plucking out the gray hairs with tweezers.

Always, she wanted a bouquet of flowers on the kitchen table where we ate. When I hiked the ranch, I tried always to bring her a bouquet of wild flowers. She especially liked the lavender flowers we called bird's beak, and when I brought her the first bouquet of the season, she was as grateful as if it had been Chanel No. 5.

Although she had never lived on a ranch before we moved to eastern Oregon, she accepted the lack of sidewalks and lawns, the coal oil lamps, the outdoor plumbing — and life without cash during the Depression. She never complained about hard times.

She never seemed to have moods. She had no bad days. I do not remember that she ever shouted at me or lost her temper. She did not criticize or belittle. Yet she must have been so tired.

We were not a demonstrative family. When, as an adult, I read a book by Beverly Cleary telling about growing up in Yamhill, she wrote that she couldn't remember her mother ever kissing her. Ours, too, was that kind of family, but I had never considered it a childhood omission. I was snug and nurtured and content. Home was a wonderful place — so that although I wanted to go away to school, when I left my cocoon I counted the days until Christmas vacation or the end of school so I could be home again.

After I married, Homer and I often talked of where we would live after he got out of the service. As we considered various locations, one of my first thoughts always was how far I would be from "home."

On Memorial Day again this year in Monument, everyone would have gone to the cemetery. They would have taken flowers — iris, snowballs, lilacs. They would have walked the cemetery and read the inscriptions on the markers and said, "Do you remember her?" and they would have recalled the days when those names were living beings.

But I was not at the cemetery in Monument on Memorial Day. I do not think I shall be there soon. And I have a feeling that my Mother understands. But some year, if I were to go to that little cemetery in Monument, I would first hike the hills to see if I could find a bouquet of bird's beaks. And those I would take to her grave.

CHAPTER 75

Stocking Up on Memories

The lonely ranch house is unoccupied now, but we are coming back for our annual three-day visit.

As we turn off Wall Creek Road onto the dirt lane that leads up to the old house, the rabbitbrush and weeds down the middle of the rutted road whip the underpinnings of the pickup. Few vehicles come this way.

There will be no light in the windows of the ranch house. Those windows are curtained now with cardboard and plywood. The yard is unkempt, littered with "pies" left by cattle and fallen limbs from the Russian olive trees planted for shade years ago by my Mother. We have come back for our annual hunting visit to the ranch, although we no longer carry guns for killing game. Rather we come to refuel memories.

We pull into the ranch house yard. All is mute. No one runs from the house shouting, "Hello, hello!"

We will not expect the ranch house to shelter us, but even before we unpack the tents, sleeping bags, camp stove, propane lanterns and jugs of water, we peer into its remains. Its doors are wired shut so cattle cannot gain entrance. We peer in at the kitchen, the gathering place for festive former meals, card games, conviviality. Its ceiling is falling in. More boards are missing from the side of the porch, whisked away by winds that come down the John Day from the Blue Mountains.

Everything has aged in this year we have been away. The ice house is gone, taken out by the John Day at flood stage. It was a historic structure. Long ago, when dour winters froze the river solid, ice was sawed and removed in big chunks, stored in sawdust in the ice house and used for lemonade and homemade ice cream when Grant County became a bake oven.

The old bunkhouse is all but gone, fallen in upon itself. It looks at us apologetically. This was my bedroom when our son Mitch, then a little kid, and I came for a week's visit with my parents. Homer and I slept in the bunkhouse when he came home from the war and visited Monument for the first time.

The chicken house, too, has caved in. No chickens scratch in the dirt and cackle proudly at each egg production.

And the barn is as lonely as the ranch house. Skinner, Bubbles, Punch and Judy no longer are housed here after their day's work.

The gates and fences sag dispiritedly, except those for keeping cattle in the proper pastures.

The family mostly is gone now, but I still think of it as the family ranch. My brother, Jack, runs cattle here. Except for us hangers-on on our annual visit, Jack's Herefords are the only visitors here at the ranch. They come to the barn for salt. Instinct tells them they need to lick these salt blocks, but when they come, we shall eye them warily. Jack says there are three bulls on the ranch: Larry, Moe and Curly. He does not think they are unfriendly but we do not intend to find out.

Nothing remains of the once-fenced garden plot where Mother picked raspberries and we ate great bowls of them for breakfast with thick cream, where new potatoes were robbed from the hill, where ruffly lettuce provided salad with bacon dripping dressing.

We busy ourselves now with setting up camp, eager to start exploring favorite old haunts. Before breakfast, our first morning in camp, we four will "hunt" the knob behind the house as we did when we had deer licenses. Mitch will leave first, taking the long hike up to the flat atop the knob. Of the four of us, I will have the best view, with vista to Hamilton, Rudeo, Courtrock, Monument Mountain and its lookout crown, with the silver chain of the John Day River far below looping through all. We will converge on the flat below the knob, comparing deer and other wildlife seen.

The deer know the game well and cooperate, as do occasional coyotes or a badger. Once, Homer and I saw a wolf.

Back at the ranch house after camp breakfast, we head upriver in the four-wheeler for the confluence of the North and Middle forks of the John Day and park on the grassy overview. Last year, an otter performed here for us. One year, on Slickear Mountain, a huge herd of elk put on a show. Another year, we heard from afar an extraordinary cacophony and knew not what it was until a massive migration of geese blocked out the sun. Indians camped here before the homesteaders came. Arrowheads and other Indian artifacts have been found here.

As we head home, leaving the confluence again to its isolation, I think that surely it will not be lonely after this interlude of visitors but can now look to its memories again.

We pass the John Day old swimming hole between Monument and the ranch, remembering how, even after summer had arrived, we gasped when we first jumped in, but always then the river warmed up to us. Occasionally on sweltering days, a lightning storm would move in and the accompanying soft shower would deodorize the sweating earth.

Each of us has his favorite haunt here in the northwestern most corner of Grant County. I will hike up Board Creek on the second day. Mitch chooses the strenuous hike to the top of Johnny Cake. Louann walks upriver, among the ponderosa pines. Homer heads down the road to the old orchard and Wall Creek. Not only do we sop up memories, but scatter more.

Because surely memories are not for humans only. Surely the old ranch house has memories from its 100-year accumulation. So, too, the old swimming hole and the confluence and the knob.

Tuesday morning, we sorrowfully load up the rigs. I walk down the road, telling everything goodbye. Homer comes along in the pickup and we head down the road.

For three days, we feasted on memories. But I sense that we were not self-centered. I sense that the ranch house and the garden spot and the barn and the knob and confluence will not be lonely after we drive away. They have their supply of memories, too.

223

CHAPTER 76

Gifts Are Not Just Material Things

The grey March morning at the hospital when Mother died, I thought how fleeting some of it had been.

It was only day before yesterday that we crowded into the tent on our new ranch. It was only yesterday that the mouse chewed a hole in my best ruby-red dress. It was this morning that our high school principal designated me as silliest girl in school.

But not everything pertaining to those years of growing up on the ranch during the Depression was ephemeral. Some of it was as indelible and continuing as days on a calendar: lessons that were learned on the ranch that would last a life time; gifts, not of a material kind.

I wished that morning that I had let Mother and Lynn know of those gifts they had given — perhaps to salve disappointment at their not being able to provide all material things, and to remind them not all gifts are of that kind.

There was the love of reading they wrapped up and gave to me one year. They taught that reading was not a waste of time although there never was a moment on that cattle ranch when some other task could not have been done. Busy though our days were, reading was regarded as a necessity. Books and magazines were a staple in our two rooms.

Our lack of cash, and the unavailability of store-bought entertainment, taught us to love and depend on the outdoors. I learned the therapy provided by a hike on the hills. That great eastern Oregon outdoors never became polluted with my problems although I dumped whatever I had in its hands when I walked the ranch.

Exploring the rimrocks, the little creeks, the falls where the bird's beaks grew, was not only unfailing entertainment but more restorative than watching a premiere showing on TV. There was never a re-run.

Living on a ranch taught us respect and love for animals, especially the dogs. We learned much from them: selfless love, companionship, and entertainment that they gave.

From Mother we learned the lessons of courage and adaptability. She came to eastern Oregon as a tenderfoot. Ranch life to her was totally new. "Light bread" was a mystery. Horseback riding a novel experience. Rubbing elbows with rattlesnakes she took in stride.

Poverty resulted in another gift — the gift of deriving pleasure from small things: a bouquet of wild brown-eyed Susans on the breakfast table. At our ranch, we were taught that there was no reason to be despondent because money was in short supply. Mother planted cheerfulness regularly and we noted that cheerfulness begets cheer. Laughing at one's predicament, if one is able to laugh, makes the predicaments of mortals somehow inconsequential compared to the overall scheme.

Then, too, the lack of money made us more dependent on people rather than things. We had no movies, no professional ball games, no operas to attend. We sought entertainment with our friends and learned the value of friendships and of the gratification those relationships can bring.

At some Christmas or birthday along the way, I was given a gift of realization: that happiness and money are not synonymous. That was a rare gift to find under a tree.

There is another gift that lack of money provided: the pleasure of work. Work on a cattle ranch was never ending. Work was as natural as sleeping or breathing. It was not something to be resisted, but to be undertaken and done, with satisfaction upon the completion. It mattered not that those jobs were often mundane.

Another gift everyone might place on his want list, year after year, was handed perfunctorily to me: happy family life.

None of these gifts or lessons will ever wear out or be thrown away.

Poverty, if poverty it was that hovered over our eastern Oregon cattle ranch while I was growing up, was not painful for me.

Printed in the United States
127320LV00002B/57/A